Age-Friendly Communities of Faith

"Kristen Miller's *Age-Friendly Communities of Faith* is a practical, thoughtful, and compelling call to action for all generations to live the words we pray and end the social isolation and neglect of the elders in our midst. Religious communities, regardless of the faith tradition, ought to be inherently intergenerational—a family of families—where both older and younger generations can learn from each other, yet churches and other houses of worship are becoming more disconnected than ever from the elders in our midst."

—**Micah D. Greenstein**, Senior Rabbi,
Temple Israel, Memphis, Tennessee

"Having been in the congregational respite ministry field for over twenty years, I wish our church had had this well written book as a resource. Kristen has done a fantastic job of highlighting the challenges of the church and its aging members and the necessary steps to ensure the retention of our pillars of the faith. With practical assessments and innovative solutions to some of the glaring challenges of aging. This is a must read for church staffs and ministry boards as well as seminarians beginning their journey within the church and community. Congratulations, Kristen. Well done!"

—**Robin Dill**, Congregational Respite Developer

"Older adults today are living longer and leading more engaged, purposeful, and health-conscious lives than ever before. But while many older adults are thriving and living well, large numbers of them face formidable challenges. In her book, Miller explores the challenges of aging and the role of faith communities. It is insightful, well-researched, and provides practical information and valuable tools for leaders of all faiths. This book is a must-read for any congregation wanting a comprehensive and compelling ministry with older adults."

—**Richard H. Gentzler Jr.**, author of *An Age of Opportunity: Intentional Ministry By, With, and For Older Adults*

"*Age-Friendly Communities of Faith* provides a compelling vision, a storehouse of relevant information and practical guidance, and life-giving inspiration for congregations that seek to be in vital ministry with people of all ages, especially those in their senior years. The book is more than a how-to resource; it is a friendly guide on a journey toward congregational transformation."

—**Kenneth L. Carder**, Ruth W. and A. Morris Williams Jr. Distinguished Professor Emeritus, Duke Divinity School

Age-Friendly Communities of Faith

A Guide on How to Serve and Retain Older Congregation Members While Maintaining Church Health

KRISTEN MILLER

Foreword by Richard F. Address

RESOURCE *Publications* • Eugene, Oregon

AGE-FRIENDLY COMMUNITIES OF FAITH
A Guide on How to Serve and Retain Older Congregation Members While Maintaining Church Health

Copyright © 2025 Kristen Miller. All rights reserved. Except for brief quotations in critical publications or reviews, no part of this book may be reproduced in any manner without prior written permission from the publisher. Write: Permissions, Wipf and Stock Publishers, 199 W. 8th Ave., Suite 3, Eugene, OR 97401.

Resource Publications
An Imprint of Wipf and Stock Publishers
199 W. 8th Ave., Suite 3
Eugene, OR 97401

www.wipfandstock.com

PAPERBACK ISBN: 979-8-3852-4641-0
HARDCOVER ISBN: 979-8-3852-4642-7
EBOOK ISBN: 979-8-3852-4643-4
VERSION NUMBER 05/30/25

This book is dedicated to members of the clergy of every faith and denomination. Thank you for your service, your teaching, your love, and your guidance. You are so very much appreciated.

"Aging is not lost youth but a new stage of opportunity and strength."
—Betty Friedan

Contents

List of Illustrations and Tables | ix
Foreword by Richard F. Address | xi
Preface | xv
Acknowledgments | xvii
Introduction | xix

Part 1: Understanding the Problems Older Adults Face
1   Falls | 3
2   Dementia | 10
3   Vision and Hearing Loss | 17
4   Social Isolation | 25
5   Caregiving | 31
6   Elder Abuse, Neglect, & Exploitation | 38
7   Relationship Challenges | 49
8   Other Challenges | 56

Part 1 Conclusion | 62

Part 2: Finding Solutions
9   Environmental Redesign | 67
10   Dementia-Friendly Faith Communities | 75
11   Communication Redesign | 85
12   Inclusive Programming | 93
13   Caring for the Carers | 100
14   Community of Watchmen | 106
15   Healing the Family | 113
16   Other Solutions | 120

Part 2 Conclusion | 128

Contents

Part 3: Challenge as Opportunity
17   Intergenerational Connections | 133
18   Healthy Aging as Ministry | 140
19   Conducting a Needs Assessment | 147
20   Analyzing Results & Effecting Changes | 164
21   Member Retention | 172

Conclusion | 179

Glossary of Terms | 183
Resources | 187
Bibliography | 195

List of Illustrations and Tables

Figure 1- What a person with macular degeneration sees | 18

Figure 2- What a person with cataracts sees | 19

Figure 3- What a person with glaucoma sees | 20

Figure 4- Chart representing how the different challenges older adults face intersect and affect each other | 62 & 128

Figure 5- Image of a door handle that is easy to use for people with disabilities | 70

Figure 6- Chart representing pictographs of universal symbols | 72

Figure 7- Image of a swing-clear door hinge | 73

Figure 8- Image of an exit door disguised to look like a bookcase | 77

Figure 9- Image representing the Hearing Loop symbol instructing users to switch to telecoil | 90

Figure 10- Image of a Little Free Pantry | 124

Figure 11- Chart representing how faith communities can provide solutions for the challenges older adults face | 129

Figure 12- Chart representing the Eight Dimensions of Wellness | 146

Figure 13- Example of a survey regarding accessibility of places of worship | 150

Figure 14- Example of a survey regarding dementia, eyesight, and hearing | 151

Figure 15- Example of a survey regarding social isolation | 152

List of Illustrations and Tables

Figure 16- Example of a survey regarding caregiving | 153

Figure 17- Example of a survey regarding elder abuse, fraud, scams, and family relationships | 154

Figure 18- Example of a survey regarding emotional health, food insecurity, housing, and transportation | 155

Figure 19- Example of a survey regarding neighborhoods and physical health | 156

Figure 20- Example of a survey regarding intergenerational connectedness and volunteer opportunities | 157

Figure 21- Example of a survey asking participants to provide demographic information | 158

Figure 22- Example of a survey regarding participation in the faith community | 159

Figure 23- Example of a survey regarding health ministry | 160

Figure 24- Example of a survey regarding health concerns and availability of resources | 161

Figure 25- Example of a survey asking participants to choose their top choices for congregational programming | 162

Figure 26- Example of a survey regarding neighborhood issues and barriers to health-related congregational programming | 163

Figure 27- Chart representing answers to survey questions recorded on a spreadsheet | 167

Figure 28- Example of a worksheet regarding SMART goals | 170

Figure 29- Chart representing the cycle of identifying challenges, identifying solutions, implementing changes, and adherence to mission | 181

Foreword

SEVERAL DECADES AGO, WADE Clarke Roof published a groundbreaking book which began the formal study of what we call the Baby Boom Generation. *A Generation of Seekers* has been followed by scores of articles, books and now, websites that have attempted to analyze and quantify this post World War II generation that has helped transform American society and spark the revolution in longevity. The vast majority of these sources have concentrated on the demographic, sociological and political impact of this generation. Very few of these have looked at the spiritual path that this generation has travelled for it has been, in many ways, groundbreaking. Thanks to the blessing of medical technology and advances in public health, the Boomers may expect to live longer and better than any previous generation. With that longevity has also come major spiritual challenges and concerns that confront not only elders, but their families as well. Aging is a multi-generational concern, and Kristen Miller seeks to examine a host of issues that impact the totality of contemporary experience from a position of how communities of faith can be an active and valuable participant.

Why are faith communities so important? Reverend Sheila Macdonald Macgregor, in her book *Redesigning Your Life: A Practical Spirituality for the Second Half of Life* notes that "It is perhaps no accident therefore that the longevity revolution parallels the spirituality wave. Boomers, for whom health is the number one concern, are discovering that the faith many of them abandoned back in the sixties and seventies may well provide the key to better physical and mental health, and that a vibrant spirituality, nurtured by a caring community, is central to a healthy ecology of body, mind and spirit." (p.169,170). The catalyst for the vibrant spirituality is the by-product of the revolution in longevity: our search for meaning. For perhaps the first time in human history, across the globe we have people living longer than ever and with that the time to contemplate the essential question of all religions: "what is the meaning of my life?" Rabbi Abraham Joshua Heschel, the famous Jewish scholar and theologian of the twentieth century discussed this in his understanding that we humans are creatures in search of meaning. Through community, ritual, prayer and service, faith communities provide a venue for elders to seek their sense of purpose and meaning.

One of the gifts of longevity that opens the dialogue on our search comes at various stages in our life's journey. It is that moment that we come to know that what we need in life is not more material possessions, but rather a sense of spiritual truth. This shift in outlook helps to transform how we live our lives, what our priorities may be and how, we interact with those around us. These are also the moments in our life that we begin to understand the reality of our own mortality and thus, we begin the process of seeking to define what our legacy may be. The various religious traditions speak to these significant issues from the perspectives of their own history, belief systems and sacred texts. But all focus on that fundamental question of helping the individual grapple with question of meaning and purpose.

Age Friendly Communities of Faith is not, however, a theoretical introspective book. Rather, it is a deeply reality-based work that raises significant questions and challenges around issues that all elders and our families face, while staying rooted in the realities and possibilities of faith. While Christian in its focus, clergy and lay leaders of other faith groups will find meaning in these chapters, for the issues are common to so many as we grow and get older. Pay particular attention to the section on "Healthy Aging as Ministry". There is a paucity of congregations who spend significant energy and resources in ministry to elders. Yes, many congregations will have "senior" groups with lunches, outings and some educational programming. But few will have a clergy (or trained volunteer) whose sole focus will be on the aging population which, in many congregations, comprise the majority of their members. The sections on Relationships and Family Issues add to the sections that deal with such everyday challenges as Caregiving, Falls, Dementia and how a congregational environment can become age-friendly.

Becoming an "age friendly" congregation will take some work and dedication on the part of leadership. However, implicit in her book is the issue of how a congregation can support and care for and empower and engage elders. A challenge that is present in almost all the current literature on aging is how we deal with the reality of time and how we manage the tensions that accompany us as we age. Time becomes ever more present and powerful for we come to understand that no matter how much we pray, we cannot control the time we have left. Thus, how we chose to spend that time becomes a spiritual choice. Do we choose to enhance and grow, or do we choose a sense of surrender. With the realities of so many living longer with a variety of chronic illnesses, the ever-present concerns around what we call the "economics of aging" and expanding reality of isolation and loneliness, there is a growing need for communities of faith to respond in personal and meaningful ways to the needs of their community. Faith communities can help each of us in our own personal search for meaning in life's mystery.

Faith communities can provide this support because they provide what all of us wish in our lives. Rabbi Jack Bemporad, writing in a Parabola Magazine Anthology called "The Inner Journey" pointed out this reality noting that all of us seek, and indeed need, reassurance, recognition and connectedness. We need to feel that our lives mean something in the grand scheme of history, that we are valuable and that our lives can and do make a difference and that we are connected, not only to our community, but to something transcendent. Faith communities can provide for these needs and do so within a context of faith and celebration.

In these moments of challenge and opportunity, faith communities can provide that sense of a safe and welcoming home that so many of us desire, a place that supports, empowers, accepts and comforts us in this most amazing part of our life's journey.

Shalom,
Rabbi Richard F Address, D.Min
Jewishsacredaging.com

Preface

One is never too old to be used by God to accomplish His specific purposes. Sacred texts show us plenty of examples of those who lived an incredibly long time who, even in their advanced age, still had a divine purpose. The book of Genesis says that Enoch faithfully walked with God for 300 years, and that Noah not only lived for 950 years, but he spent 120 years building the ark. In working with older adults, some of whom are nearing the end of their lives, I am often asked, "Why am I still here?" My answer is always, "Because you still have a purpose, and that purpose is to teach the rest of us things we need to know."

Acknowledgments

SINCERE APPRECIATION FOR THE following individuals for their advice, feedback, interviews, and survey responses that went into the writing of this book:

1. Rabbi Richard Address, Jewish Sacred Aging, Cherry Hill, New Jersey
2. Beaver Baptist Church Staff Member, Brighton, Tennessee
3. Bishop Kenneth Carder, Duke Divinity School, Durham, North Carolina
4. Robin Dill, author of *Walking With Grace*, Atlanta, Georgia
5. Rabbi Micah Greenstein, Temple Israel, Memphis, Tennessee
6. Rev. Corbin Kill, First United Pentecostal Church, Quitman, Mississippi
7. Rev. Bob Turner, Church of Christ White Station, Memphis, Tennessee

Introduction

IT'S NO SECRET THAT our population is growing older. By the year 2034, a mere decade from the writing of this book, there will be for the first time in history more people over the age of 65 than people under the age of 18. Over the years we have heard terms like "the silver tsunami" and been made aware that the Baby Boomer generation would soon be turning the page into older adulthood, but now that this issue is staring us in the face, what are we to do about it?

Here are some interesting facts about our aging population according to the Population Reference Bureau[1]:

1. In 2022, there were 58 million Americans over age 65; by 2050 that number will climb to 82 million which is a 47% increase.
2. By 2050, the number of older adults who identify as non-Hispanic white is expected to drop from 75% to 60%, making this generation of older adults the most racially and ethnically diverse than it's ever been.
3. Older adults are more educated now than they have ever been; 33% of people over 65 have a college education compared to just 5% of their predecessors in 1965.
4. Older adults are staying in the workforce longer as well; 39% of older adults are still working beyond retirement and that number is expected to increase to 41% by the year 2032.

---

1. See Mather and Scommegna, "Fact Sheet"

Introduction

5. The poverty rate for older Americans has dropped in the past 50 years from 30% in 1966 to 14% currently. However, there is wide economic disparity in people of color versus non-Hispanic whites.
6. Statistically, more older adults are able to live independently longer than their predecessors a decade ago, owing to more home modifications and assistive devices.
7. Obesity amongst older adults is higher than it has ever been, with 40% of those over 65 currently identified as obese, compared to just half of that a generation ago.
8. More older adults are divorced now than in previous decades, with 4% of men and 15% of women. That being said, the number of women living and aging alone has also increased- 27% of women ages 65–74 live alone and that percentage skyrockets to 50% of women ages 85 and older.
9. 6.9 million Americans over age 65 live with Alzheimer's and other dementias, and that number will more than double to 13 million by the year 2050.[2]

Today's older adults are changing the way we as a society think about retirement and growing older. While they still experience the same issues as their predecessors in terms of chronic diseases and loss of independence, they are also challenging the mindset that retiring means checking out of life. Modern older adults overall tend to be more active, work longer, travel, volunteer, go back to school, and generally disrupt the ageist concept that older people are frail and burdensome. However, older adults do face the realities of a body that is in the process of wearing out and those realities are the focus of this book.

Places of worship are not immune to "the silver tsunami" either and many are now re-evaluating their priorities since faith communities serve a vital role in our societal infrastructure, beyond just spiritual nourishment. Even since Biblical times, faith institutions have played multiple roles in caring for the mind, body, and spirit of believers- the elders of early Jews served as mediators in legal disputes in addition to providing spiritual support and looking after widows and the elderly; people flocked to Jesus and his disciples for both spiritual and physical healing. Today faith communities worldwide routinely care for the sick, feed the hungry, clothe the naked,

---

2. See Alzheimer's Association, "2024 Alzheimer's Facts and Figures"

INTRODUCTION

house the homeless, and run multitudes of outreach and mission projects. Communities of faith are the fabric that ties together a world of people interdependent on each other.

For decades places of worship have focused on child and youth programs so that those children will eventually grow up and take the place of today's church leaders and members, but in so doing, our older members have been largely left out of the equation to be forgotten. However, times change, and our demographics change and so the question now becomes how can we care for our older members' needs while simultaneously bringing up their future replacements?

Older adults are a treasure trove of knowledge, wisdom, and experience that is just waiting to be discovered by younger generations. By examining how the faith community can move to accommodate the needs of its older congregants, we will also be teaching younger people how to properly care for their elders and be more sensitive to their needs, while connecting the generations together to strengthen community bonds.

To understand how to better accommodate the needs of older adults, first we need to examine what unique challenges older adults face, which is covered in Part 1 of this book. Part 2 will look at practical solutions faith communities can take to mitigate those challenges, and Part 3 will dive into how to turn obstacles into opportunities to enhance church health and enable communities of faith to also be communities of connection.

It is hoped that this book will help places of worship become more sensitive to the needs of older adults and be a place that they can turn to for help, but also be a place they can turn to for overall wellness; and in turn, serve as models to younger generations on how to age well and care for those in their twilight years.

PART 1

Understanding the Problems Older Adults Face

"Even to your old age and gray hairs I am he, I am he who will sustain you. I have made you and I will carry you; I will sustain you and I will rescue you."

—Isaiah 46:4 (NIV)

1

Falls

WHEN YOU HEAR THE word falls in reference to older people, does that old Life Alert commercial come to mind? The one with the old lady on the floor saying, "I've fallen, and I can't get up?" Falls are a major threat to older adults' health, safety and independence. In fact, falls are a leading cause of fatal and non-fatal injuries in people over 65, causing hip fractures, head trauma, and death[1]. Falls are so common amongst older adults that it is estimated more than 1 in 4 older adults fall each year, and every 11 seconds an older adult is treated in the emergency room for a fall. Every 19 minutes, an older adult dies as the result of a fall[2].

There are many reasons why older adults experience falls. For one thing, as people age, they begin to lose muscle mass and bone density, so they are not as physically strong as they used to be. It also means that once a fall occurs, a fracture is more likely to happen, as well as having a more difficult time getting off the floor. Muscle mass and bone density can be increased with regular exercise and a healthy diet, which can be a challenge for many older adults. Barriers to exercise and healthy diet include factors such as a sedentary lifestyle and poor eating habits, having no immediate access to healthy foods (either by living in a "food desert", or dental problems, or mental/cognitive problems, or financial instability, etc.), having no

1. See WISQARS 2020
2. See CDC, "Facts About Falls"

immediate access to safe spaces to exercise (such as living in a non-walkable neighborhood, or living in an area of high crime, or no transportation to exercise facilities, or lack of financial resources to access exercise facilities, etc). Right off the bat, older adults are at a disadvantage in the fight against falls due to changes in the body that naturally occur with aging and significant obstacles to aging well.

Another common issue that causes falls is changes to vision. It is normal for an older adult to experience less acute vision, more problems with glare, and a need for more light due to the natural aging process. However, certain conditions like cataracts, glaucoma, and macular degeneration can cause substantial threats to a person's safety and quality of life. These conditions, which are much more prevalent in older adults, can cause a person to have more trouble seeing where they are going, or to distinguish between steps or similarly colored different surfaces. Cognitive changes can also affect a person's vision, making things appear distorted or by causing visual input to be misinterpreted by the brain.

Changes in a person's walking gait also contribute to falls. Sometimes those changes are caused by neuropathy or arthritis in the feet and legs which can make walking painful, or hard to tell where the foot is striking the ground. Sometimes those changes are caused by neurological disorders like dementia or Parkinson's, which heavily affect the nervous system and motor control areas of the brain.

Medications can significantly contribute to falls, especially since many older adults take several medications. The more medications a person takes, the higher their risk of experiencing a fall. The reasons why that happens can often be attributed to side effects like sleepiness, dizziness, or low blood pressure; interactions between prescription drugs, over-the-counter medications, supplements, and food; and because older adults metabolize medications more slowly than younger people, which can lead to a toxic buildup in the body. Thankfully there is a national movement encouraging doctors to decrease and de-prescribe medications in older adults as part of the Age-Friendly Public Health Systems model called The 4 M's- Medication, Mobility, Mentation, and What Matters. Some common medication-related fall risk culprits are:

1. Anticonvulsants –treat seizures, nerve pain, fibromyalgia, and bipolar disorder

2. Antidepressants –treat depression
3. Antihypertensives –lower blood pressure
4. Antipsychotics –reduce hallucinations, delusions, disordered thinking
5. Antispasmodics –suppress muscle spasms, both in the GI tract as well as in other parts of the body
6. Benzodiazepines –treat anxiety and sleeplessness
7. Opioids –treat pain
8. Sedative hypnotics –for short-term use to help with bedtime sleep
9. Anticholinergics- treat Chronic Obstructive Pulmonary Disease, Parkinson's Disease, allergy, vertigo, neurogenic bladder dysfunction

Many older adults cannot accurately describe what medical conditions they have, the names and dosages of their medications, or what those medications are used to treat. Sometimes medication regimens are confusing, and it is not unusual for a lot of older adults to take their medications improperly, or not at all due to the side effects, and that may lead to falls. One common complaint is from drugs used to treat high blood pressure and congestive heart failure by removing excess fluid from the body (diuretics). The biggest side effect of diuretics is having to go to the bathroom frequently, which in turn can sometimes cause falls if a person is rushing to the restroom.

Common Causes of Falls
1. Muscle weakness
2. Problems with balance
3. Changes in walking gait (shuffling of feet)
4. Neuropathy
5. Medication side effects
6. Vertigo & vestibular (inner ear) imbalances
7. Foot problems
8. Incontinence
9. Vitamin D deficiency
10. Trip hazards
11. Low or reduced vision
12. Hearing loss

> 13. Dim lighting
>
> For more information on older adult falls, and the STEADI Fall Prevention Program, visit CDC.gov.

Environmental factors are a major cause of falls as well. Things like having to go up steps or over thresholds, uneven ground and sidewalks, slippery flooring, no handrails or grab bars, certain kinds of furniture, clutter, rugs, yard debris, etc. can all cause trip and fall hazards. Out of the other causes of falls, environmental factors are the easiest to mitigate, which will be covered later in this book.

Other things that can contribute to falls include vertigo or vestibular imbalances; orthostatic hypotension (sudden drop in blood pressure on standing); foot problems including bunions, plantar fasciitis, sores, and improper/ill-fitting footwear; incontinence which can lead to rushing to the restroom; and Vitamin D deficiency.

Complications of falls range from mild to fatal. A minor fall may result in soreness or bruising; a major fall may result in broken bones, head trauma, or even death due to a head injury or an inability to get off the floor or call for help. Unfortunately, many older adults lose their lives every year because they have experienced a fall and spent several days on the floor unable to move. Broken bones, especially a broken hip, can cause serious physical and cognitive decline in older adults. Depending on their age, health conditions, and support system, surgery may not always be an option. In many cases an older adult may not even survive the surgery or anesthesia needed to repair the injury and then become bed bound. Being bed bound for long periods of time can easily result in pressure sores, infections, and pneumonia, as well as take a tremendous toll on a person's mental and cognitive health.

> People with hearing loss are nearly three times as likely to fall compared to those with normal hearing but wearing a hearing aid reduces the risk of falling by 50%. *American Geriatric Society*

In best case scenarios, an older adult who breaks a bone and survives the surgery can be a good candidate for inpatient rehab (either in a rehab hospital or skilled nursing facility, aka "nursing home"), then return home with outpatient physical and occupational therapy and home healthcare. Even so, that person faces a long convalescence and many challenges, such as hospital-acquired infections, hospital delirium, a need for increased support in the home from non-medical home care workers, and home modifications to make their space more accessible. In other scenarios, an older adult who has no family or is estranged from family is left to navigate this maze of healthcare on their own with no support.

Falls are also expensive. Medicare and supplemental insurance do not always cover all the medical costs associated with falls. A person is still responsible for their hospitalization deductible under Medicare Part A, and inpatient rehab stays are only covered up to day 100 by insurance. A person can usually receive physical therapy and occupational therapy at home on an outpatient basis (except in cases where the home is deemed inappropriate) and home healthcare nursing support for just a short period of time. Non-medical home care can help with everyday tasks such as housekeeping, preparing meals, assistance with bathing and dressing, etc. but it is not covered by insurance and must be paid out of pocket. Modifications that can help reduce falls such as grab bars, tub-to-shower conversion, shower chairs, toilet risers, and wheelchair ramps are also not covered by insurance.

There are several varied and multi-layered reasons why older adults are at a high risk for falls. Sometimes these risk factors can be lowered with lifestyle changes, or medication changes, or physical therapy, or medical intervention; and sometimes the underlying causes of falls can be a bit hazy due to the interdependence of each of these factors on the other. The complications from falls can sometimes be quite severe and lead to months of recuperation or result in a move to a long-term care facility or even death. Falls also place a large financial burden on older adults, many of whom are on fixed incomes and have limited means of obtaining the services and products necessary for better support. However, understanding falls is a key component to understanding the challenges that older congregation members face daily.

Chapter 9 will look at ways places of worship can make their buildings safer and more accessible for older adults, but here are some ways that older adults can make their own homes safer:

Bathrooms

1. Replace tubs with walk-in showers. If that is not financially feasible, a tub cut kit can lower the threshold needed to get in and out. If that

is not feasible, one can use a shower chair or transfer bench and a handheld shower head.
2. Add grab bars to the shower and by the toilet.
3. Replace toilet with a tall toilet (also called comfort height toilet) or use a toilet riser to make getting up and down easier.
4. Use non-skid mats inside and outside of the shower
5. Add nightlights

Bedrooms

1. Declutter and/or remove excess furniture so that there are clear pathways at least 36" wide
2. Eliminate throw rugs and any cords running across the floor
3. Add motion-sensor nightlights to make getting up at night easier
4. Add a bedside grab bar that fits underneath the mattress
5. Check the height of the bed to see if it is too high or too low

Living Spaces

1. Declutter and/or remove excess furniture so that there are clear pathways at least 36" wide
2. Eliminate throw rugs and any cords running across the floor
3. Use brighter light bulbs and add nightlights to hallways, kitchen, and other rooms
4. Use strips of brightly colored duct tape on the edges of steps and on thresholds between different flooring surfaces to make them more visible
5. Use chairs that have arms to make getting up and down easier
6. Make sure all steps have handrails that go all the way to the bottom

Outdoors

1. Add ramps for wheelchairs or smaller threshold ramps for a step-down
2. Make sure all steps have handrails that go all the way to the bottom
3. Repair all cracked or broken driveways and sidewalks
4. Fill in depressions and low spots hidden by grass

5. Keep a supply of salt or Ice Melt for the winter months

The STEADI (Stopping Elderly Accidents, Deaths & Injuries) initiative from the Centers for Disease Control is a great resource for information about fall prevention, as well as a source for free brochures. You can find out about STEADI on the web at CDC.gov/STEADI.

2

Dementia

IF IT SEEMS THAT more and more older adults are being diagnosed with dementia or exhibiting memory loss, it is because the number one risk factor for dementia is age. As our population ages, the rates of dementia rise accordingly. Currently about 1 in every 9 people over 65 has Alzheimer's disease, the most prevalent form of dementia[1].

What is dementia? Dementia is an umbrella term for a group of symptoms that include memory loss, problems with thinking and problem-solving, difficulty recalling words or using words correctly, problems with decision-making, changes to mood and personality, confusion and disorientation, difficulty with visual and spatial abilities, inappropriate behavior, paranoia and agitation, and other symptoms. There are several different diseases that cause dementia; Alzheimer's disease is the most common, followed by vascular dementia (when the brain does not receive enough oxygenated blood), Lewy Body dementia, Frontotemporal dementia, Hippocampal Sclerosis, and dementia of mixed causes. Other conditions that can cause dementia include traumatic brain injuries, Parkinson's disease, Huntington's disease, Wernicke-Korsakoff Syndrome, and Creutzfeldt-Jakob disease. Dementia of any of these causes is permanent, progressive, and currently there is no cure.

---

1. See Alzheimer's Association, "2024 Alzheimer's Facts and Figures"

Dementia

These diseases cause permanent damage to the physical structures of the brain, resulting in behaviors that are often difficult and frustrating for others to understand. Even if a person has not had a formal diagnosis, dementia can be characterized by behaviors such as:

1. Asking the same questions repeatedly
2. Getting lost in familiar places
3. Not being able to follow instructions
4. Becoming confused about time, people, and places
5. Making poor judgments and decisions a lot of the time
6. Problems taking care of monthly bills
7. Agitation, depression, and anxiety
8. Changes in mood and personality
9. Trouble having a conversation
10. Misplacing things often and being unable to find them
11. Challenges in planning or solving problems
12. Inappropriate behavior
13. Difficulty completing familiar tasks
14. Being paranoid and suspicious
15. Trouble understanding visual images and spatial relationships (i.e.- misinterpreting things they see and problems with depth perception)
16. New problems with words in speaking or writing
17. Hallucinations
18. Withdrawal from work or social activities

There are many risk factors for developing dementia; some can be modified by lifestyle changes, while others cannot. As previously stated, the number one risk factor is age. Other risk factors include genetics, Down Syndrome, and family history; health conditions such as high blood pressure, high cholesterol, obesity, and diabetes; education level; social isolation; head trauma (such as from a fall, collision, or other injury); sleep quality; air pollution; vitamin and nutrient deficiencies; depression or other mental illnesses; smoking and alcohol consumption; vision problems and hearing loss; and hospitalizations 2,5. If we were to take a deeper look at each of these risk factors, we could begin to understand why dementia occurs so frequently in older adults.

Dementia also carries several complications, the first being safety issues. Memory impairment can make everyday activities such as driving, cooking, walking, and living alone extremely unsafe. Traffic accidents, falls, fires, wandering out of the home, accidental poisoning, and other issues make it imperative that a person with dementia be supervised at all times. Dementia can also cause a person to be unable to take their medications properly, and fail to do personal care tasks like bathing, dressing and toileting. People with dementia often forget to eat and drink or have reduced sensations of hunger and thirst which leads to poor nutrition and dehydration; in the later stages they may develop trouble swallowing. A very common complication of dementia is pneumonia caused by aspirating food and liquids into the lungs caused by problems with swallowing. Ultimately dementia can lead to death as the brain is destroyed by disease.

> The Cost of Dementia
> 1. Total payments in 2024 for all individuals with Alzheimer's or other dementias are estimated at $360 billion.
> 2. Medicare and Medicaid are expected to cover $231 billion, or 64%, of the total health care and long-term care payments for people with Alzheimer's or other dementias.
> 3. Out-of-pocket spending is expected to be $91 billion, or 25% of total payments.

People who have dementia face a long, debilitating illness that not only affects their safety and quality of life, but it can also drain their finances. The Alzheimer's Association estimates that in 2024, costs to care for those with dementia will exceed $360 billion[2]. The cost of living with dementia is far higher than those living without it; costs for things like in-home caregivers, adaptive devices and medical equipment, increased hospital stays, adult day care, residential memory care, and skilled nursing care are not always covered by health insurance. Genworth Financial's annual Cost of Care survey estimates the average monthly cost of adult day care is $2,058 and the average monthly cost of assisted living is $5,350[2] The spouse of a person diagnosed with dementia usually faces a difficult decision between

2. See "Cost of Care By State"

keeping their loved one at home and placing them in a residential care facility, and how to afford either option. Many families living on fixed incomes have no choice but to keep their loved one at home, even though it may be more dangerous for the one with memory impairment.

Dementia is also a very socially isolating disease. Having dementia makes it very difficult to carry a conversation, remember social engagements, or process a lot of stimuli. A person with dementia often has a difficult time paying attention and being able to filter out background noise and movement from the object of their attention. Problems with interpreting visual input and having a severely reduced field of vision make it difficult to navigate unfamiliar places. Sometimes a person with dementia can feel embarrassed by not being able to remember names and faces, or by saying or doing the wrong thing; sometimes dementia can cause high anxiety or complete apathy. Many places a person used to visit, such as the park, grocery store, and even church can become unsafe and confusing places, so most often they are just stuck at home with a caregiver. Friends and family may not feel comfortable visiting anymore because they don't know how to adapt to their loved one's challenges, or seeing their loved one in decline may cause them too much emotional grief.

Another aspect of having dementia is how others in the community perceive that person. Even though great strides have been made towards awareness and understanding, there are still a lot of stigmas surrounding dementia. They can sometimes be labeled as "senile" or "crazy" by those who are uninformed and are often treated as such. Some others who may be well-meaning, but similarly uninformed may treat a person with dementia in a patronizing manner, using baby-talk and just placation instead of trying to empathize and understand. Most terrible are the ones who abuse or exploit those with dementia either out of anger, frustration, lack of training, or out of easy opportunity and bad intentions. People who have dementia are at an extremely high risk of experiencing elder abuse, fraud, and financial exploitation.

> Is it Dementia or Just "Senior Moments"? The 10 Warning Signs of Alzheimer's include:
>
> 1. Memory loss that disrupts daily life
> 2. Changes in planning or solving problems
> 3. Difficulty completing familiar tasks

4. Confusion with time or place
5. Trouble understanding visual & spatial relationships
6. New problems with words in speaking & writing
7. Misplacing things & losing the ability to retrace steps
8. Decreased or poor judgment
9. Withdrawal from work or social activities
10. Changes in mood and personality

For more information, visit Alz.org

It is important to note that there are also certain conditions that may look similar to dementia symptoms but are not actually dementia. These conditions are usually reversible or treatable, so that's why it is so important to see a doctor as soon as a person notices changes to their memory or thinking. Some of these conditions include[3]:

1. Normal Pressure Hydrocephalus (buildup of spinal fluid on the brain)
2. Medications can have different interactions due to changes in metabolism
3. Depression or other mental health disorder
4. Urinary Tract Infection can cause memory loss, confusion, delirium, etc. in older people
5. Thyroid Disease can cause memory loss or loss of concentration, sluggishness
6. Vitamin B-12 Deficiency can cause confusion, personality changes, forgetfulness
7. Diabetes can cause memory problems, confusion, irritability
8. Alcohol—binge drinking even at a younger age can cause brain cell death
9. Thiamine/Vitamin B-1 Deficiency can cause Wernicke-Korsakoff syndrome (WKS), a chronic memory disorder characterized by confusion, memory loss, hostility and agitation, sometimes brought on by heavy alcohol use.

3. See Mayo Clinic, "Dementia"

10. Transient Ischemic Attack (TIA), "Mini Stroke" can cause vascular damage in the brain
11. Dehydration from not drinking enough liquids also can cause dementia symptoms, as can electrolyte imbalances.
12. Subdural bleeding, which is bleeding between the surface of the brain and the covering over the brain can be common in older adults after a fall. Subdural bleeding can cause symptoms like those of dementia

Dementia is a scourge amongst our older population. It robs people of their memories, their independence, their plans for the future, and often, their dignity. It is an illness that is complicated, terrifying, frustrating, isolating, and terribly expensive for both the person who has dementia and their caregivers. Dementia is often misunderstood by the general public, even though nearly every person has been touched in some way by it. Thankfully there are several organizations across the globe that are actively working towards increasing awareness, education, and empathy, and researchers are diligently trying to understand the underlying causes of how cellular death and brain damage occur so that one day there might be a cure.

Chapter 10 offers practical tips for training and programs that faith communities can use to become more dementia-friendly. But here are some ways that older adults can lower their personal risk factors for developing dementia:

1. Eat a healthy diet that includes lean proteins, lots of fruits and vegetables, whole grains, and healthy fats. Limit red meat, processed foods, and sugar.
2. Exercise several times a week to improve cardiovascular health, improve mood, and create new neural pathways in the brain.
3. Manage chronic conditions such as high blood pressure, high cholesterol, and diabetes that can lead to an increased risk of strokes.
4. Quitting smoking can improve good blood flow to the brain.
5. Drink alcohol in moderation; heavy drinking can cause problems with cognition.
6. Get your vision and hearing checked to prevent cognitive decline.
7. Get good sleep because a lack of sleep can impact cognitive health.

8. Protect your head; traumatic brain injuries can substantially increase your risk of dementia. Wear a bike helmet and seat belt and take measures to prevent falls.
9. Continue to challenge your brain by learning new hobbies, taking classes, or learning about something interesting to you.
10. Stay social– being withdrawn and socially isolated can lead to cognitive decline.
11. Find healthy ways to manage stress, and talk to a doctor about anxiety, depression, and other mental health issues to lower your risk of cognitive decline.
12. Exercise your mind by working puzzles, play strategy games, and other things that involve complex tasks.

The Alzheimer's Association is a fantastic resource for information, educational speakers, and brochures. Their website is Alz.org. Other wonderful resources and further reading are included in the Resources section of this book.

Risk Factors for Dementia

1. Age- The older the age, the higher the risk factor
2. Ethnicity- African Americans and Latinos are more likely than Caucasians to have dementia
3. Gender- Women are more likely than men to develop dementia
4. Genetics & Family History- people with the APOE-e4 gene are more likely to have dementia

Alzheimer's Association. 2024 Alzheimer's Disease Facts and Figures. https://www.alz.org/media/Documents/alzheimers-facts-and-figures.pdf

3

Vision and Hearing Loss

IT'S NOT A MYSTERY that the human body experiences many changes with age; metabolism slows, the skin thins, and mechanisms begin to wear out. The same is true for the five senses and older people begin to experience the world in a different way than their younger counterparts. This chapter focuses particularly on changes that occur to vision and hearing in older adults, which can have a cascade effect on other areas of health and wellbeing.

According to the American Optometric Association, people begin to experience changes in their vision in their 40s. These normal vision changes can cause symptoms such as[1]:

1. Need for more light. As you age, you need more light to see as well as you used to. Brighter lights in your work area or next to your reading chair will help make reading and other close-up tasks easier.
2. Difficulty reading and doing close work. Printed materials can become less clear, in part because the lens in your eye becomes less flexible over time. This makes it harder for your eyes to focus on near objects than when you were younger.
3. Problems with glare. When driving, you may notice additional glare from headlights at night or sun reflecting off windshields or pavement during the day. Changes in your lenses in your eyes cause light

[1]. See American Optometric Association, "Adult Vision: 41–60 Years of Age"

entering the eye to be scattered rather than focused precisely on the retina. This creates more glare.

4. Changes in color perception. The normally clear lens located inside your eye may start to discolor. This makes it harder to see and distinguish between certain color shades.

5. Reduced tear production. With age, the tear glands in your eyes will produce fewer tears. This is particularly true for women experiencing hormone changes. As a result, your eyes may feel dry and irritated. Having an adequate amount of tears is essential for keeping your eyes healthy and for maintaining clear sight.

These changes can be coped with easily by wearing glasses or contacts, using hydrating drops, and using brighter lightbulbs. They may only be a small nuisance and not a real threat to a person's way of life. However, people over the age of 60 are at a much higher risk for developing serious eye diseases.

One such disease is age-related macular degeneration (AMD). "[It] is an eye disease that affects the macula (the center of the light-sensitive retina at the back of the eye) and causes central vision loss. Although small, the macula is the part of the retina that allows us to see fine detail and colors. Activities like reading, driving, watching TV and recognizing faces all require good central vision provided by the macula. While macular degeneration decreases central vision, peripheral or side vision remains unaffected[2]."This what a person with AMD sees:

2. See "Senior Vision: Over 60 Years of Age"

Another eye disease that affects older adults is cataracts. "Cataracts are cloudy or opaque areas in the normally clear lens of the eye. Depending upon their size and location, they can interfere with normal vision. Usually, cataracts develop in both eyes, but one may be worse than the other. Cataracts can cause blurry vision, decreased contrast sensitivity, decreased ability to see under low light level conditions (such as when driving at night), dulling of colors and increased sensitivity to glare." This is what a person with cataracts sees:

Another disease common among older adults is diabetic retinopathy. "Diabetic retinopathy is a condition that occurs in people with diabetes. It is the result of progressive damage to the tiny blood vessels that nourish the retina. These damaged blood vessels leak blood and other fluids that cause retinal tissue to swell and cloud vision. The condition usually affects both eyes. The longer a person has diabetes, the greater the risk of developing diabetic retinopathy. In addition, the instability of a person's glucose measurements over time can impact the development and/or severity of the condition. At its most severe, diabetic retinopathy can cause blindness."

Glaucoma is another eye disease that affects older adults. "Glaucoma is a group of eye diseases characterized by damage to the optic nerve resulting in loss of peripheral (side) vision. It often affects both eyes, typically one eye before the other. If left untreated, glaucoma can lead to total blindness. People with a family history of glaucoma, African Americans, and older adults have a higher risk of developing the disease. Glaucoma is often painless and can have no obvious symptoms until there is a significant loss of side vision." This is what a person with glaucoma sees:

PART 1: UNDERSTANDING THE PROBLEMS OLDER ADULTS FACE

Another severe eye disease that can occur with older age is retinal detachment. "Retinal detachment is a tearing or separation of the retina from the underlying tissue. Retinal detachment most often occurs spontaneously due to changes to the gel-like vitreous fluid that fills the back of the eye. Other causes include trauma to the eye or head, health problems like advanced diabetes, and inflammatory eye disorders. If not treated promptly, it can cause permanent vision loss."

Most of these eye diseases can be treated or reversed if caught quickly, or at a regular eye exam. However, older adults face barriers to getting annual eye exams. For one thing, eye exams are not covered by Medicare or Medicare Supplement/Medigap plans; Medicare Advantage plans do cover annual eye exams and glasses or contacts but only pay up to a certain percentage of other treatments necessary for some of these diseases. Older adults can also take out an independent vision insurance plan, but for those on fixed incomes, the cost of seeing an eye doctor and getting necessary treatments may be unaffordable. Another barrier is transportation to the eye doctor. As one can tell from the examples, vision changes caused by eye diseases can make it very difficult and dangerous to drive. There may not be accessible public transportation (particularly in rural areas), and only a small number of older adults who qualify for Medicaid also qualify for transportation to medical appointments. Some older adults may have a fear of getting treatments for these conditions done because they may involve surgery and have a complicated recovery regimen, such as having to lie face down and/or take several eye drop medications on a schedule. For those who live alone and have limited to no support, recovery may be next to impossible.

Risk Factors for Vision Problems

1. Chronic, systemic conditions such as diabetes or high blood pressure.
2. A family history of glaucoma or macular degeneration.
3. A highly visually demanding job or work in an eye-hazardous occupation.
4. Health conditions related to high cholesterol, thyroid, anxiety or depression, and arthritis for which you take medications. Many medications, even antihistamines, have vision side effects.

American Optometric Association. Eye Health for Life. "Adult Vision: 41–60 Years of Age".

Vision changes in older life also carry many health and safety complications. Safety concerns like being able to cross the street, determine the difference between food packaging and chemical packaging, the ability to take medications properly, falls, etc. could very well mean the difference between life and death. Many older adults may have to stop driving, which can lead to depression and grief over a loss of independence as well as social isolation and withdrawal from activities they once enjoyed.

Age also causes natural changes in a person's ability to hear, most often an inability to hear high-pitched noises or tones that are very close to each other or be able to hear a person speaking clearly when there is a lot of background noise. Researchers have noted that "by age 50, most people have trouble hearing noise above 14khz at all, and at average volume the top end is usually closer to 11.2khz. By age 70, the average person hears sounds up to 9.8khz comfortably at normal noise levels, with a top end of around 12khz for loud noises[3]." About half of adults over 65 have some loss of hearing.

There are two types of hearing loss. The first is sensorineural hearing loss that occurs when the inner ear or auditory nerve become damaged. The risk factors for this type of hearing loss include age, exposure to loud noises, head injuries (such as from a fall), certain medications (including blood pressure medications), or an inherited condition. Conditions such as high blood pressure and diabetes can also contribute to increased risk factors. Sensorineural hearing loss is usually not treatable medically or

3. See HEAR Center. "How Does Your Hearing Change As You Age?"

surgically, and people experiencing this type of hearing loss most often must use hearing aids. The second type is conductive hearing loss which occurs "in the outer or middle ear where sound waves are not able to carry all the way through to the inner ear. Sound may be blocked by earwax, or a foreign object located in the ear canal; the middle ear space may be impacted with fluid, infection or a bone abnormality; or the eardrum may have been injured[4]." Conductive hearing loss can usually be treated or reversed by medical or surgical means. It is also possible for people to have a mixture of both types of hearing loss.

The best way to get a handle on hearing problems is with a hearing exam, but just like as in the case with vision loss, there are barriers to getting hearing exams. Medicare and Medicare Supplement/Medigap plans also do not cover hearing exams. Medicare Advantage plans cover the cost of a basic exam and a percentage of the cost of hearing aids. To be truly effective, hearing aids need to be fitted by an audiologist who can help the person with hearing loss make the best choice; unfortunately, those hearing aids can cost thousands of dollars.

> Common Objections to Hearing Aids
>
> 1. "My hearing's not that bad." Hearing aid users wait, on average, 10 years before getting help for hearing loss. But during that time, communication with loved ones becomes more difficult, and isolation and health risks increase.
> 2. "Wearing hearing aids means I'm old, and I'm not ready for that." Plenty of people with a hearing impairment sit silently rather than joining in conversations and activities, because they fear that hearing problems will make them seem helpless or less than competent.
> 3. "I heard that hearing aids are difficult to use." That's why most doctors and hearing centers include a trial period, so you can be sure the type you've chosen—whether it's a miniature behind-the-ear model or one that fits into your ear—is right for you.
>
> Johns Hopkins Medicine. "The Hidden Risks of Hearing Loss".

---

4. See Johns Hopkins Medicine, "Types of Hearing Loss"

Vision and Hearing Loss

Another barrier to getting hearing exams is that many older people don't realize they've lost hearing abilities and resent being told they need an exam and potential hearing aids. Some signs that a person needs to have their hearing checked by a doctor include[5]:

1. Difficulty understanding consonants and digraphs like "sh" and "ch"
2. Difficulty with following conversations, especially in crowds
3. Challenges with talking on the phone
4. Complaints about the volume of the TV or radio
5. Problems with balance
6. Problems remembering things that were said
7. Challenges with keeping attention

Hearing loss can also present health hazards and complications to a person's way of life. Significant safety concerns like the ability to hear a fire alarm or tornado siren, or dizziness and balance issues that can cause a fall, have the potential to be life and death matters. The inability to understand conversations can lead to social isolation and withdrawal from enjoyable activities, leading to depression. However, the most troubling complication of hearing loss is its potential to cause problems with cognition; several studies have pointed to an important link between hearing quality and dementia[6].

Although it is normal for older adults to experience some loss of acuity in vision and hearing, very high percentages of people over 65 are at risk of developing serious conditions which can have detrimental consequences on their health, safety, and independence. Regular examinations to watch for early signs are key, but come with obstacles, such as cost, lack of transportation, fear, and denial. Yet understanding these challenges is vital to understanding the challenges older adults face every day.

Chapter 11 focuses on ways that faith communities can help older congregation members who have vision and hearing problems by adjusting their oral and written communications. But here are some quick tips that older adults can use to cope with hearing and vision loss at home:

---

5. See Graves, "10 Signs of Hearing Loss You Shouldn't Ignore".
6. See Lin, "Hearing Loss and the Dementia Connection".

Part 1: Understanding the Problems Older Adults Face

Vision

1. Get regular annual eye exams to monitor for changes and adjust prescription
2. Switch to brighter LED bulbs throughout the home, add lamps to dim areas, and add nightlights
3. Ask for anti-reflective coating on your glasses or sunglasses, purchase anti-glare or anti- blue light screen protectors for computers and devices
4. Use hydrating eye drops
5. Increase contrast by using felt-tip pens or Sharpies to write lists
6. Switch to large print books or audio books
7. Use GPS to help with driving

Hearing

1. Get a hearing evaluation to check for problems
2. Use sound amplifiers or hearing aids as necessary
3. Use smoke detectors/carbon monoxide detectors that flash and have a bed vibrator
4. Use earplugs or hearing protection when doing yardwork or being around loud noises
5. Talk to your pharmacist about medications that can cause hearing loss
6. Switch to a captioned telephone and TV closed captioning
7. Turn your cellphone to vibrate for incoming calls and texts

The National Institute on Aging has many free brochures and booklets available in bulk on several topics, including vision and hearing loss. To order, visit Order.NIA.NIH.gov

4

Social Isolation

THE TERM "SOCIAL ISOLATION" has been thrown about quite a bit in the wake of the Covid-19 pandemic. While we all collectively suffered from social isolation to some degree, it was particularly devastating to older adults; people who did not have anxiety, depression, or memory loss prior to the pandemic started experiencing symptoms on a widespread scale, and those who did have those conditions experienced physical and mental decline at a much faster rate. Even prior to the pandemic, social isolation was already a curse amongst older adults, the negative health effects comparable to smoking a pack of cigarettes a day *and* having alcoholism[1].

How is social isolation even defined? "Loneliness is the feeling of being alone, regardless of the amount of social contact. Social isolation is a lack of social connections. Social isolation can lead to loneliness in some people, while others can feel lonely without being socially isolated."[2] For this purpose, we will focus more on the quantitative and qualitative aspects of social isolation, rather than the more subjective feelings of loneliness.

According to a 2020 report from the National Academies of Sciences, Engineering, and Medicine, about 25% of adults over 65 were socially isolated, meaning they had very few social connections. However, a more

---

1. See Freedman and Nicolle, "Social Isolation and Loneliness"
2. See Centers for Disease Control, "Loneliness and Social Isolation"

recent 2023 national poll indicated that number is now closer to 34%[3] Things that contribute to social isolation include having to stop driving, loss of a spouse, family living far away, having dementia, having mobility impairments, vision and hearing loss, caring for a family member, having to withdraw from activities and hobbies, being an immigrant, identifying as LGBTQIA+, and other risk factors. The "digital divide" also caused an increase in social isolation. While the world pivoted to online formats during the pandemic, older adults were by and large left out. Using new technologies, accessing computers and tablets, and even accessing internet services was, and still is, beyond reach for those who are more used to an analog world. For many older adults, their only social interaction comes from doctors' appointments.

Older adults who are socially isolated tend to be the ones who get forgotten by their former social networks. A common situation is a person who had to withdraw from activities and social groups to take care of a spouse; once that spouse passed away, the person was then in declining health themselves and unable to rejoin groups who had moved on without them. In some cases, social isolation occurs when a person starts physically declining, but refuses help out of embarrassment or pride; sometimes mental health issues can be a contributing factor in this case. Even though we are now post-pandemic, many older adults are still afraid of catching Covid-19 and self-isolate out of fear.

The health implications of social isolation are staggering:

1. Social isolation significantly increased a person's risk of premature death from all causes, a risk that may rival those of smoking, obesity, and physical inactivity.
2. Social isolation was associated with about a 50% increased risk of dementia.
3. Poor social relationships (characterized by social isolation or loneliness) were associated with a 29% increased risk of heart disease and a 32% increased risk of stroke.
4. Social isolation is also associated with an increase in risk of anxiety, depression, and suicide.

Because there is such a strong connection between the mind and the body, it is thought that being socially isolated on a chronic basis activates

---

3. See Flowers et al., "Medicare Spends More on Socially Isolated Older Adults"

a "biological defense system" that can increase inflammation on a cellular level. Dr. Steve Cole at the Social Genomics Core Laboratory at the University of California, Los Angeles stated that, "Loneliness acts as a fertilizer for other diseases. . .the biology of loneliness can accelerate the buildup of plaque in arteries, help cancer cells grow and spread, and promote inflammation in the brain leading to Alzheimer's disease. Loneliness promotes several different types of wear and tear on the body."[4]

Common Causes of Social Isolation

1. Disability
2. Living alone
3. Limited finances
4. Impaired mobility
5. No family close by
6. Never having married
7. Transportation challenges
8. Divorced, separated, or widowed
9. Inability to remain physically and mentally active
10. Lack of access and inequality due to rural living or being part of a marginalized group
11. Poor health and well-being including untreated hearing loss, frailty, and poor mental health
12. Societal barriers such as ageism and lack of opportunities for older adults to engage and contribute

Kate Benesch, 2020. "Causes of Social Isolation in Older Adults", GriswoldCare.com.

Health implications aside, some of the complications of being socially isolated include safety issues like falling and not being able to get help; a person's home falling into disrepair and becoming unsafe because they don't have anyone to call on for help; being food insecure because they don't have transportation to the grocery store or know how to navigate online shopping; hoarding behaviors to fill the emotional void of isolation; failure to do personal care tasks such as bathing or household cleaning tasks due to fear of falling or lack of strength; and being a victim of a scam or fraud.

Social isolation is also costly- a study in 2017 estimated that it costs Medicare around $6.7 billion in annual spending due to increased

---

[4]. See National Institute on Aging, "Social Isolation"

treatments, medications, and hospitalizations needed to manage the health conditions that are worsened by social isolation, because without good social networks, socially isolated people tend to seek "crisis-driven care"[5] What that federal spending means for the individual is an increase in monthly Medicare Part B premiums which are normally taken from a person's Social Security, in addition to their deductibles. Another cost aspect of social isolation is having to move to senior living or a nursing home, which often occurs when there's been a catastrophic illness or fall exacerbated by being socially isolated.

> Facts on Social Isolation
> 1. Loneliness increases the likelihood of mortality by 26%
> 2. People who are lonely report 5% more severe symptoms in the common cold than those who are less lonely.
> 3. 18% of adults aged 65 and older in the U.S. live alone, and 43% report feeling lonely on a regular basis.
> 4. Between 10% and 43% of community-dwelling seniors are socially isolated.
> 5. Lonely seniors have a 59% higher risk of physical and mental health decline.
>
> Kate Benesch, 2020. "Causes of Social Isolation in Older Adults", GriswoldCare.com.

Social isolation is a multi-layered issue, often with more than one cause, that can be very detrimental to an older adult's health, independence, and quality of life. Oftentimes they become "invisible" to all those except with whom they have some limited contact, such as a doctor or mail carrier. Socially isolated older adults may have weak social relationships to begin with, perhaps due to family estrangement or mental health issues, or their social relationships may have withered due to death of friends or their own declining health. Whatever the cause, the complications can be severe and very expensive, not to mention the fact that these are precious human beings who have lived full lives as contributing members of society who are now forgotten about in their old age. Social isolation is not just a curse for

---

5. See Mikhail, "1 in 5 Older Adults"

Social Isolation

older adults, but it robs the rest of us of the joy of knowing and learning from them.

Chapter 12 identifies key ways that faith communities can decrease social isolation through inclusive programming that appeals to older adults across a wide spectrum of ages and stages, but here are some practical tips that older adults can use on their own to help combat social isolation:

1. Take the Connect2Affect.org Social Isolation Assessment Quiz to find out more about your personal risk factors and potential health consequences.
2. Keep a journal to better understand your thoughts and feelings to improve your mental health and relationships.
3. Think about what friendship means to you and what things you are really looking for in a friend.
4. Practice the art of active listening to boost your conversational confidence.
5. Keep a mental list of helpful conversation starters when trying to make new connections.
6. Rekindling connections with relatives and old friends can go a long way towards boosting your mood and reducing isolation.
7. Meet new people who share similar interests. Places to try might include:
    - Senior Centers and Community Centers
    - Libraries
    - Places of Worship
    - Support Groups
    - Volunteer Opportunities
    - Civic Organizations, such as Rotary, Toastmasters, Lions Club, etc.
    - Book Clubs, Supper Clubs, Bridge Clubs, Chess Clubs, etc.
    - YMCA
    - Community Choir, Band/Orchestra, or Theatre
    - Make an effort to meet your neighbors

Part 1: Understanding the Problems Older Adults Face

- Front Porch Community's Well-Connected Program lets you engage with people all over the country by phone or computer for free (see Resource section)
- Call the Institute on Aging's Friendship Line 24/7 at 1-800-971-016
- Use the National Eldercare Locator or your local information number (2-1-1 in some areas) to find opportunities in your neighborhood.

5

Caregiving

CARING FOR THE CHANGING needs of older adults is a big business; there are more professional caregiving companies in the United States than there has ever been, and the demand for paid caregivers is so great that legislation has been proposed to make it easier to import workers from other countries; by 2031 the American Immigration Council predicts professional caregivers will the largest occupation in the country[1]. However, the biggest segment of caregivers is not paid. They are the family, friends, and neighbors that provide informal caregiving networks to millions of older adults every day.

Just how big is the caregiving issue? Here are some facts and figures from the *Caregiving in the U.S.* report compiled by the National Alliance on Caregiving and AARP:

1. The number of unpaid caregivers rose from 43.5 million in 2015, to 53 million in 2020. That number is continuing to climb as approximately 10,000 Baby Boomers turn 65 every day.
2. 79% of caregivers are caring for a person age 50 and older
3. 24% of caregivers are providing care for more than one person
4. 26% of caregivers say they have difficulty coordinating medical care
5. 26% are caring for a person with Alzheimer's disease or another dementia

---

1. See Bulos, "Caring for Aging Parents"

6. 23% say that caregiving has made their own health worse
7. 61% of caregivers are women, 39% are men
8. 34% of caregivers are part of the Baby Boomer generation, while 29% are Gen-X, and 23% are Millennials
9. 45% of caregivers have had at least one financial impact as a result of providing care
10. 61% are working and caregiving at the same time[2].

The types of tasks that caregivers perform fall into three categories: Activities of Daily Living (ADLs) which include walking, bathing, dressing, feeding, toileting, and transferring (standing to sitting, bed to chair, etc.); Instrumental Activities of Daily Living (IADLs) which include shopping, transportation, handling finances, housekeeping, managing medications, and managing communication (phone, mail, etc.); and Medical Tasks such as ostomy care, oxygen, blood pressure and blood sugar monitoring, scheduling medical appointments, assessing pain levels, and other tasks. In short, caregivers do it all.

Many caregivers suddenly find that role thrust upon them out of necessity, and it can be a complete change in their way of life that sometimes includes relocating, selling or buying a house, and leaving a job. What's more is that there is no manual on how to be a caregiver; the role is often taken on during a time of crisis and the medical community offers very little in the way of guidance or care navigation through the complex maze of medical appointments, medication regimens, and equipment. Some caregivers, such a spouse, gradually take on more and more responsibility until their caregiving tasks become a 24/7 job. Other caregivers, often referred to as "the sandwich generation" are both caring for an older adult as well as their children.

Caregiving can take an enormous toll on a person's emotional health. In a 2023 article for the *Los Angeles Times*, Gemma Bulos writes of her experience as a caregiver: "Like many people in our situation, we found that our parents, once the pillars of our family, suddenly relied on us for their very existence. We feel critically ill-equipped for a huge responsibility that is taking an immense toll on our mental and emotional well-being. Despite being in the company of countless others facing similar challenges in our generation, we have an overwhelming sense of aloneness. Caregivers often

---

2. See National Alliance on Caregiving, "Caregiving in the U.S. 2020 Report"

grapple with a loss of identity, strained relationships and scarcity of time to rest and recreate."

> Many caregivers of older adults are themselves growing older. The average caregiver of a recipient 65 years of age or older is 63 years old. Of these caregivers, one third report being in fair to poor health. Administration on Aging. (2005). NFCSP: Complete Resource Guide

The *Caregiving in the U.S. 2020* report corroborates the abundant anecdotal evidence of caregivers all over the country. Even caregivers who had both paid and unpaid outside help reported feeling alone in their journey, and 36% indicated that caregiving has caused them high emotional stress. One of the complications of caregiving is caregiver burnout, where a person reaches a point that they are so mentally exhausted by the never-ending task list that they begin to neglect or even mistreat their care recipient. Very few doctors ever assess for caregiver burnout, even though there are multiple tools available, as well as medical billing codes so that they can be reimbursed by insurance companies.

> Cost of Caregiving
>
> 1. At $470 billion in 2013, the value of unpaid caregiving exceeded the value of paid home care and total Medicaid spending in the same year, and nearly matched the value of the sales of the world's largest company, Wal-Mart ($477 billion). AARP Public Policy Institute. (2015). Valuing the Invaluable: 2015 Update.
> 2. Family caregivers spend an average of 24.4 hours per week providing care. Nearly 1 in 4 caregivers spends 41 hours or more per week providing care. National Alliance for Caregiving and AARP. (2015). Caregiving in the U.S.

Another complication of caregiving is that it is so physically demanding that the caregiver's health begins to fail before their care recipient's health. More than 1 in 5 caregivers report having difficulty caring for their own health, and the groups most likely to have a harder time managing their own health include those people who are caring for a spouse, those who are caring for someone with Alzheimer's or another dementia, and people from lower household incomes. All of those groups also indicate that their health has declined since becoming a caregiver.[3] Why is that? Caregivers overall tend to be stretched thin between caring for all or most of another person's needs, managing their own households, and work obligations. There simply aren't enough hours in a day to do all the things that need to be done, especially when that caregiver has no other help.

Caregiving can also be very expensive. The average cost for a paid professional caregiver is around $25-$30 an hour, and most companies require 4-hour minimums of care. Adult daycare averages $95 per day. If a caregiver must work an eight-hour day and their care recipient is unable to be left alone all day, it can cost $100-$240 per day for care. For households that make less than $80,000 a year, the cost of professional caregiving is simply too high. The financial impact of caregiving has caused people to stop saving money, take on more debt, use up their short-term savings, pay bills late or not at all, and/or borrow money from family or friends. Oftentimes, a caregiver must stop working to care for their loved one, which incurs a critical loss of income to the household.

Signs of Caregiver Burnout

1. Emotional and physical exhaustion.
2. Withdrawal from friends, family and other loved ones.
3. Loss of interest in activities previously enjoyed.
4. Feeling hopeless and helpless.
5. Changes in appetite and/or weight.
6. Changes in sleep patterns.
7. Unable to concentrate.
8. Getting sick more often.
9. Irritability, frustration or anger toward others.
10. If someone is contemplating self-harm or suicide, they can call or text the Suicide & Crisis Lifeline at 988

For more information, visit My.ClevelandClinic.org

Adult day care and non-medical home care (which provides essential assistance with both ADLs and IADLs) are not covered by insurance. In some cases, both services may be partially subsidized by a state's Medicaid Waiver program which seeks to provide care for a person at their home

3. See Family Caregiver Alliance, "Caregiver Statistics: Demographics"

rather than in a more expensive skilled nursing home, but those dollars are stretched very, very thin in states that have not passed expanded Medicaid legislation. In states that have expanded Medicaid, some are also able to pay family caregivers who are unable to work due to their caregiving responsibilities[4]. Expanded Medicaid is part of the Affordable Care Act which matches federal spending with a state's newly expanded Medicaid-eligible population. As of the writing of this book, 9 states, primarily those in the southeast, still have not passed legislation to expand Medicaid[5].

Short-term respite, in which a person can stay in an assisted living facility or memory care facility for a few days or weeks, is also not covered by insurance unless that person is on hospice care. Respite care can be a very valuable asset to caregivers who need to travel out of town or who need to recuperate from an illness or surgery, but for those with mid-low incomes, it is simply unaffordable.

One payment tool that can be used to pay for professional caregivers is the VA Aid and Attendance program. It is open to veterans and their spouses (even if the veteran is deceased), who have served during a wartime period and meet other eligibility criteria. It can be a tricky and difficult process to get approved, so those who may qualify need to use an attorney or other service provider who is very knowledgeable about the Veterans Administration processes. However, if approved, a household can receive an extra $1200-$1400 a month to pay for in-home caregivers, adult daycare, assisted living, memory care, or skilled nursing facility.

Caring for an older adult is a complex issue that takes a heavy toll on one's emotional health, physical health, and finances. In many households, adult children are expected to care for their aging parents' needs but are ill-equipped to do so due to a lack of training, and due to their parents' failure or inability to plan ahead for their own caregiving needs. In some households, adult children are faced with providing care for their parents from a distance, relying on paid professionals to fill in the gaps. Still other households have no family and must rely on friends or neighbors to attend to their needs. Nationwide there is a monumental shortage of professional caregivers, and many barriers to accessing government-subsidized or insurance-covered care in addition to skyrocketing costs for care.

Chapter 13 dives into three categories of service to help caregivers- education, support, and respite- but here are some ways that caregivers in

4. See Mohamed et al., "Pandemic-Era Changes"
5. See Kaiser Family Foundation, "Status of State Medicaid"

your congregation can care for themselves and prevent burnout and physical decline:

1. Ask for and accept help. Make a list of ways in which others can help you. Then let them choose how to help. Ideas include taking regular walks with the person you care for, cooking a meal for you and helping with medical appointments.
2. Focus on what you can do. At times, you might feel like you're not doing enough. But no one is a perfect caregiver. Believe that you're doing the best you can.
3. Set goals you can reach. Break large tasks into smaller steps that you can do one at a time. Make lists of what's most important. Follow a daily routine. Say no to requests that are draining, such as hosting meals for holidays or other occasions.
4. Get connected. Learn about caregiving resources in your area. There might be classes you can take. You might find caregiving services such as rides, meal delivery or house cleaning.
5. Join a support group. People in support groups know what you're dealing with. They can cheer you on and help you solve problems. A support group also can be a place to make new friends.
6. Seek social support. Stay connected to family and friends who support you. Make time each week to visit with someone, even if it's just a walk or a quick cup of coffee.
7. Take care of your health. Find ways to sleep better. Move more on most days. Eat a healthy diet. Drink plenty of water.
8. See your health care professional. Get the vaccines you need and regular health screenings. Tell your health care professional that you're a caregiver. Talk about worries or symptoms you have.
9. Keep the faith. Pray, read scriptures, meditate, keep a journal, listen to spiritual songs– whatever your faith journey looks like for you– can bring comfort.
10. Find moments of joy. It is easy to get focused on caregiving tasks and to-do lists. Look for ways to make meaningful connections with your loved one to laugh and enjoy one another.

Caregiving

Resources and Info for Caregivers

1. National Council on Aging- NCOA.org
2. Eldercare Locator Directory- Eldercare.ACL.gov
3. National Institute on Aging- NIA.NIH.gov
4. Family Caregiver Alliance- Caregiver.org
5. Rosalynn Carter Institute for Caregivers- RosalynnCarter.org
6. Next Avenue- NextAvenue.org
7. Additional resources are located in the Resources section of this book.

6

Elder Abuse, Neglect, & Exploitation

ELDER ABUSE IS A terrible topic to discuss, but it is a topic that needs to be discussed more and brought out into the open. Older adults are at a very vulnerable stage of life where they are more dependent on others for care and are at an extreme disadvantage when trying to decide between what is fraud and what is legitimate.

> For every 1 reported case of abuse, as many as 57 more cases go unreported. *U.S. Department of Justice*

How is Elder Abuse defined? According to the CDC, "Older person abuse is an intentional act or failure to act that causes or creates a risk of harm to an older adult. An older adult is someone aged 60 or older." It is a very prevalent issue that affects at least 1 in 10 older adults[1] and recent reports indicate prevalence doubled to 1 in 5 during the Covid-19 pandemic[2]. There are several categories of abuse which are defined by the National Center on Elder Abuse:

1. Physical Abuse—the intentional or reckless use of physical harm or physical coercion that may result in bodily injury, physical pain, or impairment. Under the Older Americans Act, "physical harm" means bodily injury, impairment, or disease. Examples include but are not

1. See Centers for Disease Control and Prevention, "About Abuse of Older Persons"
2. See National Center on Elder Abuse, "What is Elder Abuse?"

limited to: Hitting, beating, pushing, shaking, slapping, kicking, pinching, and burning; Unlawful, excessive, or unnecessary use of force like restraints or force-feeding; Over-medication or under-medication.

2. Sexual Abuse- non-consensual sexual contact of any kind with an older adult. Examples include but are not limited to: Unwanted touching, sexual assault or battery, sexual harassment; Sexual interaction with elders who lack the capacity to give consent.

3. Emotional / Psychological Abuse- the infliction of anguish, pain, or distress through verbal or nonverbal acts. Examples include but are not limited to: Verbal assaults, insults, threats, intimidation, humiliation, isolation, and harassment.

4. Neglect- the refusal or failure of a caregiver or fiduciary to fulfill any part of a person's obligations or duties of care to an older person. The Elder Justice Act defines neglect as "the failure of a caregiver or fiduciary to provide the goods or services that are necessary to maintain the health or safety of an elder." Examples include but are not limited to: Failing to provide for life necessities such as food, water, clothing, shelter, and medicine.

5. Financial- the illegal, unauthorized, or improper use of an older person's resources for monetary or personal benefit, profit, or gain, or that results in depriving an older person of rightful access to, or use of, benefits, resources, belongings, or assets. Examples include but are not limited to: Misusing or stealing an older person's money or possessions; coercing or deceiving an older person into signing any document such as a contract or will; improper use of conservatorship, guardianship, or power of attorney. Note: Fraud and scams are characterized by acts perpetrated by a stranger or someone outside of a trust relationship. Deceit or misrepresentation are used to convince another to relinquish their money, property, or assets. Fraud and scams will be discussed later in this chapter.

6. Self-Neglect- an adult's inability, due to physical or mental impairment or diminished capacity, to perform essential self-care tasks. Examples include but are not limited to: Obtaining adequate food, water, clothing, shelter, personal hygiene, medical and mental health care, and safety precautions, and/or managing one's finances; Self-neglect excludes a situation in which a mentally competent older person, who understands the consequences of their decisions, makes a conscious

and voluntary decision to engage in acts that threaten their health or safety as a matter of personal choice- this is called the Right of Self-Determination.

7. Abandonment- the desertion of an older person by an individual who has assumed responsibility for providing care for an elder, or by a person with physical custody of an elder. A few state statutes classify abandonment as a separate and unique form of elder abuse. Definitions vary by state. Some state statutes categorize elder abandonment as a type of elder neglect. Abandonment may occur at a hospital, nursing home, or other public place.

Elder Abuse is a global crisis. Here in the United States, more than 643,000 older adults were treated in the emergency department for nonfatal assaults and over 19,000 homicides occurred from 2002 to 2016. Since the majority of older adults (90%) live at home in the community as opposed to living in a congregate setting, most incidents of elder abuse occur in the community. However, those living in congregate settings are more likely to report abuse[3]. Capturing accurate data can be hard to obtain because elder abuse tends to be under-reported; it is estimated that for every 1 reported case of abuse, as many as 57 more cases go unreported. People living in rural and tribal areas are also less likely to report incidents of elder abuse.

Risk Factors for Elder Abuse
1. Chronic medical conditions and poor physical health
2. Functional disability and dependence
3. Mental health problems
4. Cognitive deficits
5. Financial dependence
6. Lower socioeconomic status
7. Substance misuse
8. High levels of stress and poor coping mechanisms
9. Prior exposure to trauma
10. Limited social support / isolation
11. Poor relationship between the victim and the perpetrator

For more information, please visit the National Center on Elder Abuse at NCEA.ACL.gov

---

3. See U.S. Department of Justice, "Elder Abuse Statistics"

Who are the ones who are most likely to be a victim? Anyone can be a victim, but certain factors can increase a person's risk, such as chronic medical and mental health conditions; cognitive impairment; physical, financial, and emotional dependence; history of poor family relationship between older adult and caregiver; caregiver burden; social isolation; lack of access to support and resources; substance abuse or misuse; lower socioeconomic status; high levels of stress and poor coping mechanisms; and prior exposure to trauma. Other factors that can increase a person's risk of being victimized include being female, being African American, being a younger older adult, and lacking adequate access to healthcare[4]. Elder abuse also has severe long-term consequences for victims. "The trauma of elder abuse may result in health issues such as a deterioration in health, hospitalization and increased mortality, clinical issues such as depression and suicide, social issues such as disrupted relationships, and financial loss, all leading to diminished independence and quality of life."Other consequences include feelings of shame and guilt; loss of self-esteem and compromised sense of self-worth; physical and cognitive decline; loss of attachment to the perpetrator who may be a family member caregiver; emotional distress, loneliness, isolation, and Post-Traumatic Stress Disorder; physical trauma; as well as malnutrition and dehydration.

There are also risk factors for perpetrators of elder abuse which can include chronic medical conditions and poor physical health; mental health problems; cognitive deficits; financial dependence; substance misuse; high levels of stress and poor coping mechanisms; negative attitudes towards the older adult; low social support; and early childhood abuse. Perpetrators and the types of abuse they commit vary widely, but on average they are more likely to be under 50 years old, male, Caucasian, have low education levels, be unemployed, be unmarried, have a history of childhood abuse or trauma, misuse substances, have a mental illness, have a criminal record, have interpersonal relationship problems, cohabitate with the victim, have financial problems, and be socially isolated. Adult children and spouses make up many perpetrators, but elder abuse can also happen at the hands of other family members, friends and acquaintances, paid caregivers, and strangers.

Prevalence of Elder Abuse

1. Studies have found that at least one in 10 community-dwelling older adults experienced some form of abuse in the prior year.

4. See National Center on Elder Abuse, "Research, Statistics & Data"

2. A recent meta-analysis assessing the global prevalence rates of the abuse of older women found that one in six experienced abuse in the prior year.
3. In several different studies, psychological abuse was most common, followed by physical abuse.

National Center on Elder Abuse NCEA.ACL.gov

Self-neglect also falls under the umbrella of elder abuse. It is characterized by poor personal hygiene/not bathing or taking care of hair and nails; poor medication management or refusing to take medications; evidence of dehydration, malnutrition or other unattended health conditions; unsanitary/very unclean living quarters and/or hoarding; signs of unpaid bills, bounced checks or utility shut offs; evidence of missing adequate food in the house or signs of weight loss[5]. A lot of the time those who self-neglect have cognitive or mental health issues that prevent them from caring for themselves properly. Legally if another person has Power of Attorney for a person who can no longer make sound decisions, they have the authority to step in and help the person obtain the necessary medical care and support services to get proper care. If no one has Power of Attorney, a petition for guardianship or conservatorship must be made to the court to protect the person from harm. However, there are situations wherein an older adult chooses to live that way. The Right of Self-Determination guarantees individuals the right to make their own choices. As long as an individual meets certain criteria, they are free to live as they please. The criteria are:

1. Be an adult over the age of 18
2. Be capable of knowing the difference between right and wrong; mentally competent
3. Be capable of knowing the risks and consequences of their own behavior; intellectually competent
4. Not causing harm to another person

Sometimes people choose to live in less-than-ideal circumstances. If they are fully aware of the risks of their decisions, and not suffering from dementia or a mental illness or other disease that impairs their ability to think and reason, and their behavior is not jeopardizing someone else's health and safety, they are free to live as they choose. In either case, a person may

5. See "Recognizing Self-Neglect"

be very resistant to accepting help or getting the proper cognitive and psychological assessments needed to test decision-making capacity.

> Why is elder abuse underreported? "Underreports may be caused by a number of factors including an older person's fear of retaliation by the offender, reluctance to disclose the incident because of shame or embarrassment, concern they will be institutionalized, dependency on the offender, and an inability to report because of physical limitations or cognitive impairments." National Center on Elder Abuse. 2024. "Prevalence of Elder Mistreatment".

The procedure for reporting suspected cases of elder abuse and neglect includes making a report to your local police department and/or your state's Adult Protective Services or calling 911 in the event of an emergency. Reporters should be prepared to provide as much information as possible about the alleged victim, alleged perpetrator, and the abusive situation, even if one does not know all the answers or have proof of abuse; a report can be made anonymously. While every state has statutes on reporting suspected elder abuse and neglect, not every state has Mandatory Reporting. In some states, only physicians are required by law to report, and in other states, any person working with older adults in any capacity, including clergy, are required to report[6]. Even if reporting is not legally mandated, those working with older adults should have an ethical obligation to make a report and may do so anonymously to protect their own identity from retribution, or to circumvent confidentiality.

Scams and fraud fall under the broad category of financial exploitation, and while anyone can be a victim, older adults are particularly vulnerable to this insidious threat to their wellbeing. In 2023, 101,000 victims aged 60 and over reported scams and fraud to the FBI, and older adults lose more than 3 billion dollars each year. Scams and fraud take many forms, and here are the most common ones according to the FBI[7]:

1. Romance scam: Criminals pose as interested romantic partners on social media or dating websites to capitalize on their elderly victims' desire to find companions.

---

6. See American Bar Association, "Adult Protective Services"
7. See Federal Bureau of Investigation, "Elder Fraud"

2. Tech support scam: Criminals pose as technology support representatives and offer to fix non-existent computer issues. The scammers gain remote access to victims' devices and sensitive information.
3. Grandparent scam: A type of confidence scam where criminals pose as a relative—usually a child or grandchild—claiming to be in immediate financial need.
4. Government impersonation scam: Criminals pose as government employees and threaten to arrest or prosecute victims unless they agree to provide funds or other payments.
5. Sweepstakes/charity/lottery scam: Criminals claim to work for legitimate charitable organizations to gain victims' trust. Or they claim their targets have won a foreign lottery or sweepstakes, which they can collect for a "fee."
6. Home repair scam: Criminals appear in person and charge homeowners in advance for home improvement services that they never provide.
7. TV/radio scam: Criminals target potential victims using illegitimate advertisements about legitimate services, such as reverse mortgages or credit repair.
8. Family/caregiver scam: Relatives or acquaintances of the elderly victims take advantage of them or otherwise get their money.
9. Health scams- focus on seniors because they're more likely to suffer from specific health problems. This makes them prime targets for fake remedies that promise to do a variety of things. This also includes medical brace scams, genetic testing scams, and COVID-19 scams.
10. Social Security Scams- In December 2018, the Social Security Administration warned of an upsurge in calls from con artists posing as SSA employees. Sometimes, they even use spoofing technology to make it appear the call is coming from the SSA's real phone number.
11. Counterfeit Prescription Drugs- The rising cost of prescription drugs has put a squeeze on seniors, who tend to take more of them than the average person. To save money, some seniors look for cheaper versions of their meds at online pharmacies.
12. Fake Anti-Aging Products- there are also counterfeit versions of many cosmetics and other "anti-aging" products.

13. Funeral Fraud- Some of the most vicious scams are the ones that prey on the recently bereaved. Thieves obtain info from obituaries for identity theft or to collect bogus debts.
14. Investment Scams- There are many types of investment scams, from Ponzi schemes to pump-and-dumps, that target anyone who has money to spend. However, the SEC has identified several scams that tend to focus on seniors in particular. These include: charitable gift annuities, "risk-free"/"high return" investments, phony CDs & bonds, promissory notes, sale & leaseback contracts, high-pressure sales and prime bank schemes.
15. Reverse Mortgage Scams- can involve mortgage relief, phony investments, house flipping and home repairs.

Costs of Scams

1. Scams targeting individuals aged 60 and older caused over $3.4 billion in losses in 2023—an increase of approximately 11% from the year prior. The average victim of elder fraud lost $33,915 due to these crimes in 2023.
2. Investment scams were the costliest kind of elder fraud in 2023. These schemes cost victims more than $1.2 billion in losses last year.
3. More than 12,000 victims aged 60 and over indicated that cryptocurrency was "a medium or tool used to facilitate" the scam or fraud.

Federal Bureau of Investigation. Elder Fraud, In Focus. April 30, 2024.

Scammers target older adults more than any group because they tend to be more trusting and polite, they typically own their home, usually have good credit, and typically have money in savings. Other risk factors for being a victim of scam or fraud include age- people over age 80 report losing the most money, around $1500 on average; social isolation makes people more likely to answer unknown phone numbers which is a very effective method for scammers; those with cognitive problems are less able to judge what is legitimate and what is not; and being frugal or living on a fixed income makes people more likely to fall for free or easy money.

No matter the type of scam, one thing that they all have in common is eliciting an emotional response. Whether that comes from a threat of physical harm, prosecution, computer virus, or of loss of income, or promise of a fulfilling relationship, more money, or vacation, all scamming methods play on a person's emotions and express a sense of urgency so that the victim can't take the time to think things through or talk to someone else about the situation. Scammers often instruct the victims not to tell anyone or to fabricate a story if anyone asks questions, making it even more difficult for an outsider to intervene.

Older adults are also less likely to report being a victim of a scam, often out of shame and embarrassment, or because they feel their children will think they can't be trusted to handle their own affairs. They are also less likely to know how or to whom to make a report and may not be able give very much detailed information about the scammer.

> Risk Factors for Scams
>
> 1. Dependence on others as a result of impaired functional ability or frailty.
> 2. Generational & cultural beliefs that decision-making authority rests with others.
> 3. Limited social network/social isolation
> 4. Depression & anxiety
> 5. An overly trusting nature
> 6. Dementia
> 7. Medical conditions that impair a person's thinking and judgment, including medications that cause drowsiness
>
> Karen Relmers, MD. 2023. "Why Are Older Adults More Vulnerable to Scams?" *Psychology Today.*

Elder abuse, neglect, and exploitation is a very complex, very broad, very under-reported, and very real threat to an older adult's health and well-being that can have devastating consequences, ranging from emotional and mental distress, physical and cognitive decline, hospitalizations and early death, loss of income and assets, and a much lower quality of life. These threats can be nuanced and influenced by a person's relationship with the perpetrator and could involve the threat of retaliation if brought to light. Elder abuse, neglect, and exploitation is also very expensive costing consumers billions of dollars in unrecoverable assets, along with costs associated with the legal and healthcare ramifications. Moreover, the fact that these types of abuse happen to vulnerable older adults points to ageist concepts that perceive older adults as frail, burdensome, and expendable, rather than the precious jewels of society that they are.

Chapter 14 focuses on ways that communities of faith can disrupt cycles of elder abuse, fraud, and exploitation through education, awareness, and interventions. However, there are things individuals can do to reduce their personal risk factors of being a victim:

1. Be aware that elder abuse and scams can happen and educate yourself on your risk factors and current scams going around.
2. Staying connected socially, through family and friends, places of worship, support groups, and formal services such as healthcare and mental health can reduce your risk of experiencing elder abuse.
3. Challenge ageist stereotypes by reframing aging in a more positive light to dispel the misconceptions people have about getting older.
4. Plan ahead for your future needs with documents such as Advanced Directives, Powers of Attorney, Wills, and Trusts. Be very careful about who is selected to carry out your legal and financial wishes should you become incapacitated.
5. Locate caregiving resources to prevent abuse that happens as a result of caregiver burnout and neglect.
6. Be aware of the tactics used by scammers to illicit an emotional response- a problem or a prize, a sense of urgency, instructions not to tell anyone or to make up a lie, ask for money up front to collect a prize- when in doubt, just hang up.
7. Block unwanted calls and text messages.
8. Don't give your personal or financial information in response to a request that you didn't expect.
9. Stop and talk to someone you trust before you act on the scammer's request for money or personal/financial information.
10. Purchase security software for your computer and keep it updated.
11. Don't download any apps on your phone or tablet that you didn't personally research and seek out.
12. Don't answer unfamiliar phone numbers; just let the call go to voicemail.

Part 1: Understanding the Problems Older Adults Face

The Federal Trade Commission has free print publications on a variety of topics related to scams and fraud. They are located at FTC.gov > Bulk Publications (bottom of page).

7

Relationship Challenges

MANY OLDER ADULTS EXPERIENCE dramatic changes in their relationships with family and friends. Modern families are far more mobile today than they were in previous generations and it's not unusual for members to be spread out all over the country and in other countries. In years past, families stayed together and often had multiple generations in very close proximity, if not under the same roof. While that is still the case in other cultures, Americans tend to value individualism and autonomy and that mindset is not lost on older adults either, who oftentimes prefer to stay in their own homes and live alone.

The book, *You and Your Aging Parent* by Barbara Silverstone and Helen Kandel Hyman has been a handbook for adult children in the "sandwich generation"- that is caring for older parents while also caring for their own children- since it was first published in 1976[1]. The book takes a deep dive into the complicated emotions of both adult children and their older parents.

> CBS News asked people, how often should you call your mother? "Thirty-five percent think once a week is enough, though just 12% think it's okay to call your mom once a month or less." *CBS Sunday Morning, May 8, 2016*

The book states that for older parents, emotional challenges that can put a strain on relationships with their adult children can fall into four

---

1. See Silverman & Hyman, *You and Your Aging Parent*

main categories: 1. Being overly independent and refusing help, perhaps because they truly don't need help or are deluded/in a state of denial/lack self-awareness about their own capabilities; 2. Being perfectly capable of managing their own affairs, but are pseudo-helpless- that is making unreasonable demands for time and attention or exaggerating their infirmities; 3. Being manipulative and/or pitting family members against each other, or using self-belittling tactics to gain sympathy, or using money to buy affection or punish family members; 4. Reluctance to talk about their own old age and mortality and refusal to make decisions in preparation for their future care and eventual death.

Silverstone and Hyman point out that the motivations for these types of behaviors vary. Some older adults have always had some of those personality traits, such as the manipulative father who dangles money like a carrot on a stick to make his children do what he wants them to do, or the domineering mother that makes her children feel as though they can never measure up to her standards. Some older adults have a difficult time coming to terms with old age or lack knowledge about what is normal for aging and become overly fearful, anxious, self-pitying, or dramatic. Other older adults may be in denial or lack self-awareness of how much help they actually need and actively push away their children's offers to help. In some cases, which is fairly common amongst older adults with dementia, they may develop anosognosia, a term which means they have lost the ability to be self-aware of their own limitations. And yet others are too afraid to face the fact that they are aging and will eventually die and develop a warped sense that by not discussing it, it won't happen.

For adult children, *You and Your Aging Parent* highlights the emotional challenges that can strain their relationships with their parents. Challenges such as unresolved feelings and insecurities from childhood; emotional tugs of war between love and affection and old family wounds; guilt over their own mixture of feelings or perceived failings; the balancing of work responsibilities, duty to their own families, and obligations to aging parents; fear and grief caused by watching their parents' physical and cognitive decline; not understanding the natural aging process and what is normal; fear of facing their parents' mortality; assuming they know what is best for their parents and that their parents can't possibly make the best decisions for themselves; and feelings of jealousy and sibling rivalry for affection and financial gain.

Relationship Challenges

What Causes Tension Between Parents & Children?

1. The assumption of a quid pro quo- parents believe they are entitled to a payback due to their involvement in their child's life.
2. Disappointment in partner choices due to prejudices or rigid beliefs over what constitutes a good partner.
3. Disagreements with life choices, particularly if a parent defines their personal success by the successes or perceived failures of their children.
4. Criticism of the adult child's child-rearing.
5. Comparing adult children to their siblings, relatives or others.
6. Labeling disagreements as showing disrespect for the parent's authority.

Peg Streep, 2022. "6 Sources of Tension Between Adult Children and Their Parents", *Psychology Today*. PsychologyToday.com

Even the most loving families can still experience relationship problems, sometimes just from a failure of parents and children being on the same page and making informed decisions together. Families face uncharted waters when it comes to aging because there are more choices than ever before, plus the fact that people are living longer than they ever have before. There is a lot of often conflicting information available on the internet that families didn't have a generation ago; that information overload, plus the influence of friends, neighbors, and relatives can often lead to poor family decision-making.

Another emotional challenge that affects families is grief. While grief certainly occurs after a death, grief can "accompany any event that disrupts or challenges our sense of normalcy or ourselves. This includes the loss of connections that define us"[2] Older adults may grieve their loss of ability or good health, the loss of their home and neighborhood, or even grieve the loss of the image of what they thought their retirement years would look like. Adult children may grieve the loss of a parent, the loss of their childhood home, or grieve while watching their parents' decline. Grief isn't just one feeling, but an entire range of feelings that can be expressed in different ways, such as sadness, anger, depression, hostility, anxiety, sleep

---

2. See Cleveland Clinic, "What is Grief?"

disturbances, irritability, guilt, and more. Moreover, there are different types of grief that are all just as complex:

1. Anticipatory grief occurs before an actual loss, such as when a person has a terminal illness, or a family watches their loved one move through the stages of dementia.
2. Abbreviated grief follows a shorter timeline, mainly because a person has put in "emotional labor" leading up to the actual loss.
3. Delayed grief occurs when a person can't mentally and physically process the loss until a later time.
4. Inhibited grief involves repressing emotions because a person can't recognize or process all of the confusing emotions of grief and loss. This type of grief may present as panic attacks, anxiety, insomnia, and even upset stomach.
5. Cumulative grief involves grieving multiple losses in a relatively short amount of time. It's not unusual for older adults to grieve the loss of a spouse, the loss of their family home, and the loss of their freedom simultaneously.
6. Collective grief can occur after major life-changing events like natural disasters, pandemics, wars, etc. Rather than being a personal grief, "as a group, we grieve the shared experiences we've lost as we struggle to imagine a changed future".
7. Absent grief may occur when a person is frozen in denial, or unable to show outward signs of grieving.
8. Ambiguous loss can occur when there's no closure and may also be more likely to occur in those caring for a person with dementia.
9. Disenfranchised grief can happen over a loss that society doesn't think is valuable, such as the loss of a pet or an old school pal.
10. Traumatic grief happens when someone is processing a loss and trauma at the same time, such as from an accident, natural disaster, or violence. This may result in Post-Traumatic Stress Disorder.

While it is generally accepted that there are stages of grief- denial, anger, bargaining, depression, and acceptance- not all people experience those stages nor experience them in a linear fashion. There are also some physical and behavioral symptoms that can accompany loss. Physical symptoms like fatigue, upset stomach, headaches, heart palpitations, joint pain, appetite changes and sleep disturbances, and behavioral symptoms such as confusion, trouble making decisions, hopelessness, and loss of focus can all signal that a person is grieving. Sometimes older adults and their children may be grieving a loss and not even recognize their feelings as grief; an older adult who is grieving the loss of their health and ability may appear resentful and resistant to care when an adult child is just trying to help.

> Tips for Maintaining Boundaries
>
> 1. Maintain the house rules of your adult children, even if you don't particularly agree.
> 2. Make the terms abundantly clear if you are gifting or loaning financial assets.
> 3. Avoid showing favoritism by treating all adult children and grandchildren equally, including by way of time/involvement and money.
> 4. Keep your opinions to yourself.
> 5. Your child (or your parent) is not your pal. .
>
> Peg Streep, 2024. "Why Parents and Adult Children Must Maintain Boundaries" *Psychology Today.* PsychologyToday.com

Family estrangement is another complex layer in which parents or adult children cease contact for one reason or another. Those reasons can vary widely, such as a falling out over a disagreement or emotional abuse at the hands of the other. According to an article from GreatSeniorLiving.com[3], other reasons include:

1. Conflicting expectations regarding family roles
2. Differences in values
3. Neglect
4. Problems related to mental health issues
5. A traumatic family event
6. Divorce
7. Issues related to in-laws

[3]. See GreatSeniorLiving.com, "Grown Children Who Ignore Their Parents"

Part 1: Understanding the Problems Older Adults Face

8. Issues related to marriage
9. Political disagreements
10. Disapproval of sexuality or religion
11. Judgments about career and relationship
12. Substance abuse
13. Financial stress

"In addition, some seniors feel that recent years have seen an increase in entitled adult children who stop talking to their parents for selfish reasons. But many adult children disagree with this sentiment and present a counterargument: Older parents don't recognize that their adult children have their own busy lives and that life has changed since those parents were their children's age."Estrangement can take an immense emotional toll; about one-third of parents estranged from their children contemplate suicide, and the feelings are akin to grief- more specifically to ambiguous loss.

The emotional challenges on the parts of both older adults and their adult children can have dramatic, traumatic, and long-lasting effects on decisions for care, estate plans, and family dynamics. The strain of a child meeting the demands of a parent can put a strain on the child's own marriage and relationship with their children; the strain of a parent feeling as if they are a burden to their children can cause them to underexaggerate their true needs until all is revealed in a crisis. Unresolved deep-seated feelings can cause parents to make unfavorable estate plans that cause their children undue amounts of stress; children may react to their own unresolved insecurities and have problems establishing boundaries with both their parents and in other relationships. Children who think they know best may push their parents into moves and decisions that are ultimately harmful, and parents who refuse to listen may put themselves in unsafe positions. All of these issues and many others further complicate the complex obstacles that older adults face daily.

Chapter 15 discusses techniques for opening up lines of communication and managing expectations so that families can overcome common squabbles, but here is some advice from Focus on the Family on ways older adults can heal rifts in relationships with their adult children[4]:

---

4. See Daniel, "Family Estrangement"."

Relationship Challenges

1. Initiate Change. Consider that your goal is to reconcile and restore the relationship, and not to determine who was right or wrong. If you desire the relationship to change, then be the first to work toward reconnection.
2. Walk in Humility. Parents must move forward with humility and put the relationship first.
3. Find Common Ground. You and your adult children don't have to agree on everything, but you can agree on some things.
4. Choose Affirmation. When parents lay aside their opinions and meet their adult children where they are, kids know they're loved and respected as individuals.
5. Let Go of Control. Listen more and speak less.
6. Take the Time Needed. While there isn't a cookie-cutter answer for reconciling a parent-child relationship, or how to build trust, this restoration almost always takes longer than a parent may want.

8

Other Challenges

OLDER ADULTS FACE MANY challenges in what has traditionally been called "the golden years". In addition to all the other challenges previously mentioned, this chapter looks at three more- food insecurity, housing insecurity, and transportation- and how those challenges intersect with each other.

Food insecurity is characterized not just by a lack of food, but a lack of *available* food. This encompasses the rising costs of groceries which has forced many older people to cut back on what and how much they consume, as well as the distance one must travel to reach a grocery store. Residential areas that do not have a grocery store within a 1–2-mile radius are considered a food desert. Food insecurity also encompasses factors such as a person's ability to shop and transport food home. Feeding America's "The State of Senior Hunger in America" 2021 Report concluded that 5.5 million, or 7% of older adults were considered food insecure; persons of color were nearly 4 times as likely as their Caucasian counterparts to experience food insecurity; and more than 7 million older adults are expected to be food insecure by the year 2050[1].

The factors that influence food insecurity include poverty (the average Social Security monthly payout is $1700); lack of affordable housing which causes a person to not have enough money left over to afford food; chronic health conditions, which can incur high medical bills and a more difficult

---

1. See "The State of Senior Hunger"

Other Challenges

time getting to the store; and systemic discrimination against those who are marginalized[2]. The negative consequences of being food insecure include malnutrition and poorly managed chronic conditions such as heart disease and diabetes; emotional stress like anxiety and depression; and threats to well-being such as social isolation, stigma, and shame.

A study published in a 2018 volume of *InnovAging* looked at a predominantly African- and Caribbean-American community centered in an urban food desert and compared its older adults to its younger adults in terms of food insecurity. The study found that "Both groups showed similarities by gender, ethnicity, living situations, and distance to supermarkets, but significant differences by income, functional ability, and physical limitations...More older adults had difficulty walking 10 blocks, climbing stairs, and "other physical limitations" affecting food-seeking...Higher rates of "medical conditions" affecting diet were also noted...The majority in both groups said they could "walk to a large supermarket", but older adults were less able to get food home for a variety of reasons. While food deserts are typically defined by distance to full-service markets, this study suggests that older adults face other obstacles to food security and that other community-based interventions and policies are needed to support aging in a food desert[3]."

There are some federally assisted programs to help address food insecurity. One of those is the Supplemental Nutrition Assistance Program (SNAP), formerly known as food stamps. Older adults who have $1250 or less in monthly income may be eligible, however, they may only receive the bare minimum in benefits of around $23 a month. The Commodity Supplemental Food Program or "Senior Food Box" provides a monthly food package of shelf-stable items such as canned vegetables, dried beans, cereal, canned meat, rice, etc. worth about $50. However, commodities are not available in every area, and one has to go in person to sign for and pick up the items. The Senior Farmers' Market Nutrition Program provides $5-$10 vouchers to older adults who qualify, but the program is not available in every state. Many farmers who set up stands at farmers markets also refuse to accept vouchers because the reimbursement for them from the government is difficult. The Emergency Food Assistance Program sends shelf-stable food to states for distribution to municipal and regional food banks, which all have their own criteria for eligibility. Meals on Wheels America is a national non-profit organization that uses funding from the

---

2. See National Council on Aging, "Get the Facts on Food Insecurity"
3. See Costley, "Aging in A Food Desert"

Part 1: Understanding the Problems Older Adults Face

Older Americans Act and other donors to deliver free/low-cost cooked meals to older adults, however it is also not available in many areas and several areas have long waiting lists; for example, the Meals on Wheels program in Memphis, Tennessee has a waiting list of 3,000 older adults. Now with federal spending and the federal workforce being drastically reduced, these programs are in danger of being cut back even further.

Hunger Quick Facts

1. Food insecurity is greater among minority older adults. As a result of systemic racism and discrimination, Black, Hispanic, and Native American older adults have higher rates of food insecurity.
2. In 2022, nine out of 10 of the states with the highest rates of senior food insecurity were in the South, with Louisiana having the highest rate (14%).
3. Multigenerational households are twice as likely to experience food insecurity, and older adults living with grandchildren are more likely to prioritize the children's nutritional well-being before their own.
4. Older adults with disabilities are twice as likely to be food insecure as their non-disabled peers.

National Council on Aging, "Get the Facts on SNAP and Senior Hunger" 2024.

Housing insecurity is also a major issue for older adults. While luxury senior living residences have been popping up like mushrooms, housing that is affordable for mid-low-income older adults is shrinking. For older adults who are ready to divest themselves from a house, the seemingly only options are luxury independent living or assisted living, or HUD subsidized housing. HUD (Department of Housing & Urban Development) subsidized housing is for people whose income is considered low or very low; low income is no more than 80% of the median income for the city or county in which you live, while very low-income is no more than 50% of the local median income. The figures vary by location[4]. HUD subsidized housing can be a wonderful tool for those who qualify, with many apartment communities offering on-site laundry, common areas, on-site social workers, and even congregate meals; however, there is a nationwide shortage of these affordable units, with many having waitlists for as long as

---

4. See Fivecoat-Campbell, "Trapped in the Affordable Housing Gap"

five years. Luxury senior living has many merits for those who can afford it, such as the option to age in place across different levels of care on the same campus; those communities are called Continuing Care Retirement Communities and offer independent, assisted living, memory care, and sometimes skilled nursing all in one place. Amenities can include swimming pools, fitness rooms, theatres, libraries, and the like. However, some may also require large buy-ins at the front end.

But what about the people in between? Those whose incomes are too much to qualify for HUD subsidized housing and not enough to afford luxury living? There is very little in the way of housing for middle-income older adults, such as apartments and condominiums, and what is available is often not handicapped accessible. Housing developers also are not incentivized to build more affordable housing and labor and materials costs keep going up. And this issue will only get worse over time; an independent study from the University of Chicago indicated that "the number of middle-income older adults will have nearly doubled between 2014 and 2029, from 7.9 million to 14.4 million".

How Has Housing Affordability Changed?

1. Among those buying a home, home prices combined with interest rates have risen 40% since 2021.
2. Among those renting, a record number of renters are experiencing housing cost burden—defined as spending more than 30% of gross income on housing costs—in the United States as of 2022.
3. Where you live plays a part- home prices in West Virginia are roughly 30 percent below the national average; home prices in California are roughly 90 percent above the national average.
4. Unlike other federal entitlement programs, that are available to anyone who meets eligibility criteria, there is not nearly enough funding to provide vouchers to every individual and family who qualifies for a Housing Choice Voucher (Section 8).

RAND.org. "The U.S. Housing Crisis Explained: What Americans Need to Know". September 11, 2024

The affordability of housing is in a very precarious place. The Department of Housing and Urban Development reported that "roughly one-third of people aged 50 and over overpay more than 30% of their incomes for housing—making them "rent burdened"[5]. The rising cost of rent and lower availability of affordable housing is causing a growing problem of elder homelessness. According to the National Alliance to End Homelessness (NAEH), 138,098 adults over the age of 55 were homeless and nearly 1 in 4 people experiencing unsheltered homelessness (living in places not meant for human habitation) were over the age of 55 during the 2023 annual Point-In-Time Count. Furthermore, they estimate that "homelessness among older adults is expected to nearly triple in 2030, and the population of adults aged 65 and older experiencing homelessness is anticipated to grow from 40,000 to 106,000"[6].

The reasons why older adults become homeless are varied. According to the NAEH, root causes can "include community-level factors such as lack of accessible and available housing and limited safety net resources. They also may include individual risk factors, such as medical problems, health-related behaviors such as substance use disorders, social factors (e.g., social isolation, barriers to transportation), and financial insecurity. At the same time, housing is unaffordable and the costs of necessities like healthcare leave older adults further at risk of poverty and homelessness. Adults who experience homelessness for the first time before age 50 tend to have had adverse experiences, substance use disorders, or mental health challenges; have been involved in the justice system; and/or were underemployed early on in life. On the other hand, those who first experience homelessness at age 50 and older typically have experienced a financial or health crisis, lost a loved one, or otherwise experienced a relationship breakdown with the income-earner, and/or experienced barriers to continued ability to work."

Some solutions to the affordable housing dilemma can come with their own barriers to access as well. One solution is called Accessory Dwelling Units—or ADUs—(a.k.a. "granny pods"), which are usually small houses built in the backyard of an existing house. The 2022 Housing Supply Action Plan called for more ADUs nationwide, especially for low- and moderate-income people, with pilot programs for federal ADU loans; however, many communities do not allow ADUs in their building and permitting codes.

Transportation is also a challenge for older adults. Some have had to give up driving due to problems with eyesight and other health conditions,

---

5. See Eisenberg, "New Solutions"
6. See National Alliance to End Homelessness, "Who Experiences Homelessness"

OTHER CHALLENGES

and those who live in poverty may not be able to afford a vehicle, gas, and insurance. Some cities are very fortunate to have good, reliable public transportation that incorporates different methods of travel like buses and light rail; other cities struggle to even have a bus service. Rural and tribal areas usually have no public transportation available. While nearly every place has handicapped-accessible, door-to-door transportation available, oftentimes it is reserved only for medical appointments. Some Medicare Advantage Plans and clinics sponsored by those plans offer free transportation to medical appointments, and some senior centers may offer transportation to their facilities. The current state of public transportation is woefully underprepared to accommodate the 25.5 million Americans who have travel-limiting disabilities. However, the Department of Transportation is working to enhance accessibility under the Bipartisan Infrastructure Law[7].

Food insecurity, housing insecurity, and transportation are each complex, multi-layered issues in and of themselves, but each influences the others. And in turn, each issue impacts a person's overall well-being. Some human rights, like the right to adequate shelter and food, can become luxuries in later life; getting from one place to another which used to be so easy it was taken for granted, can become a major hurdle to overcome. But like with the other challenges that have been presented, understanding these issues is the key to understanding the obstacles that millions of older adults face every day.

Chapter 16 examines different ways that faith communities can act as safety nets when it comes to food, housing, and transportation insecurity. For people that are experiencing these issues, there are some places to seek out information about local resources, such as calling 2-1-1 or going to 211.org to access local directories, or by calling their local Area Agency on Aging, which can be located at Eldercare.ACL.gov or by calling 1-800-677-1116.

---

7. See U.S. Department of Transportation, "Accessibility"

Part 1 Conclusion

SO FAR IN PART 1, this book has explored 11 different challenges facing older adults: falls, dementia, vision loss, hearing loss, social isolation, caregiving, elder abuse, relationship issues, food insecurity, housing insecurity, and transportation. When taken into context within the big picture of aging, the golden years can start to look more like the bleak years. While many, many older adults are thriving in retirement and resetting standards for aging well, many more of their counterparts are struggling. Out of all the eleven issues presented, four of them stand out as the "worst of the worst"- falls, dementia, relationship issues, and social isolation.

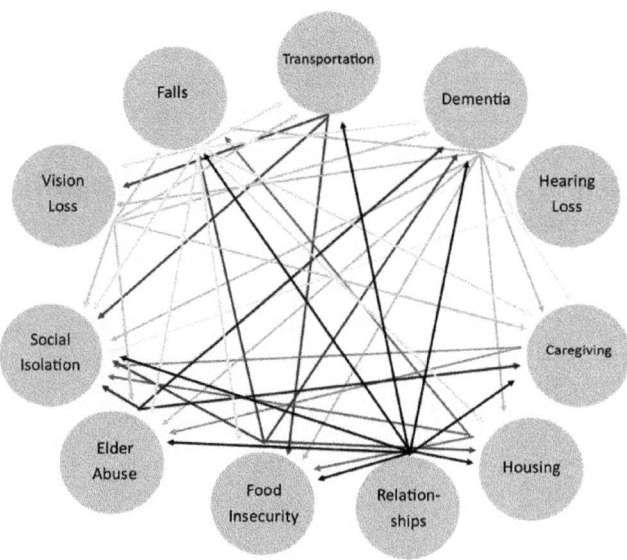

Part 1 Conclusion

This chart represents how each factor has a direct impact on the others. For example, a lack of transportation has a direct impact on food insecurity, particularly if a person lives in a food desert; hearing and vision loss each have a direct impact on both social isolation and an increased risk of developing dementia; inaccessible housing impacts one's fall risk and unaffordable housing directly impacts likelihood of food insecurity, etc. Each one of the 11 identified challenges of aging is a multidimensional issue influenced by other equally complicated issues, such as legislation, eligibility criteria, inflation, workforce shortages, breakdown of family and social networks, the aging process, outdated and underperforming infrastructure, personal bias and systemic biases, and a host of other social ills. However, knowledge is power when it comes to finding unique and creative solutions that can help our older adults flourish and be treated as valuable human beings deserving of dignity and respect.

PART 2

Finding Solutions

"Gray hair is a crown of splendor; it is attained in the way of righteousness."
—Proverbs 16:31 (NIV)

9

Environmental Redesign

THE WORDS "ACCESSIBILITY" AND "inclusive design" have been thrown around a lot lately as more and more people are becoming increasingly sensitive to the needs of those with special abilities. Playgrounds are now becoming more adaptable so that children with special needs aren't left on the sidelines; street crossings and airplanes are being redesigned to better accommodate the needs of those who use wheelchairs; beaches are renting out all-terrain, sand-safe motorized scooters; all over the country a whole new world is opening for those to whom many things were a locked door.

Places of worship shouldn't be left out of the equation either. When the Americans with Disabilities Act (ADA) was made law in 1990, buildings all over the country went through a retrofitting process to meet the accessibility requirements of the new law. Wheelchair ramps, marked handicapped parking spaces, handrails, wheelchair accessible bathroom stalls, lowered water fountains, braille signage, and many other changes took place[1]. Once those changes were made, they were mostly taken for granted. However, over the years another concept was formed that takes ADA to a new level- Universal Design.

Universal Design is defined as "The design of products and environments to be usable by all people, to the greatest extent possible, without the need for specialized design", and broadens the perspective of the ADA

---

1. See U.S. Dept. of Transportation, "Accessibility"

design standards with a more holistic approach. Universal Design is based on 7 principles[2]:

1. Equitable Use- The design is useful and marketable to people with diverse abilities.

    a. Provide the same means of use for all users: identical whenever possible; equivalent when not.

    b. Avoid segregating or stigmatizing any users.

    c. Provisions for privacy, security, and safety should be equally available to all users.

    d. Make the design appealing to all users.

2. Flexibility in Use- The design accommodates a wide range of individual preferences and abilities.

    a. Provide choice in methods of use.

    b. Accommodate right- or left-handed access and use.

    c. Facilitate the user's accuracy and precision.

    d. Provide adaptability to the user's pace.

3. Simple and Intuitive Use- Use of the design is easy to understand, regardless of the user's experience, knowledge, language skills, or current concentration level.

    a. Eliminate unnecessary complexity.

    b. Be consistent with user expectations and intuition.

    c. Accommodate a wide range of literacy and language skills.

    d. Arrange information consistent with its importance.

    e. Provide effective prompting and feedback during and after task completion.

4. Perceptible Information- The design communicates necessary information effectively to the user, regardless of ambient conditions or the user's sensory abilities.

    a. Use different modes (pictorial, verbal, tactile) for redundant presentation of essential information.

2. See The R.L. Mace Universal Design Institute, Universal Design Principles

Environmental Redesign

    b. Provide adequate contrast between essential information and its surroundings.

    c. Maximize "legibility" of essential information.

    d. Differentiate elements in ways that can be described (i.e., make it easy to give instructions or directions).

    e. Provide compatibility with a variety of techniques or devices used by people with sensory limitations.

5. Tolerance for Error- The design minimizes hazards and the adverse consequences of accidental or unintended actions.

    a. Arrange elements to minimize hazards and errors: most used elements, most accessible; hazardous elements eliminated, isolated, or shielded.

    b. Provide warnings of hazards and errors.

    c. Provide fail safe features.

    d. Discourage unconscious action in tasks that require vigilance.

6. Low Physical Effort- The design can be used efficiently and comfortably and with a minimum of fatigue.

    a. Allow user to maintain a neutral body position.

    b. Use reasonable operating forces.

    c. Minimize repetitive actions.

    d. Minimize sustained physical effort.

7. Size and Space for Approach and Use- Appropriate size and space is provided for approach, reach, manipulation, and use regardless of user's body size, posture, or mobility.

    a. Provide a clear line of sight to important elements for any seated or standing user.

    b. Make reach to all components comfortable for any seated or standing user.

    c. Accommodate variations in hand and grip size.

    d. Provide adequate space for the use of assistive devices or personal assistance

Part 2: Finding Solutions

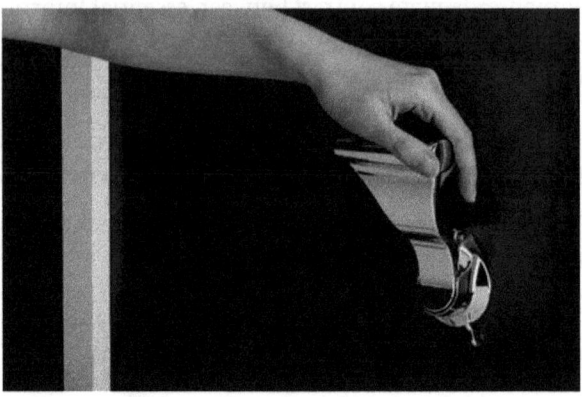

This door handle is easy-to-operate and requires less range-of-motion

So how can the Universal Design principles be put into action for faith communities? The answers may be simpler than you might think, and not only will making these suggested changes be much more accommodating to your older adult members, other members and visitors may find the changes beneficial as well. In addition, implementing changes for ease of use also translates into the added benefit of safety, which in turn can lower your institution's risk of liability.

> Quick Ways to Improve Your Parking Lot
> 1. Get clarity on the issues; use videos to identify problem areas and traffic flow.
> 2. Get team members out there to greet guests, direct traffic, & provide assistance.
> 3. Increase signage to make entrance, exits, and directions clearer.
> 4. Add an additional worship service if attendance is at capacity.
> 5. Resurface & restripe; a civil engineering firm may help you redesign to increase spaces, safety, & efficiency.
>
> Rich Birch, 2020. "5 Ways to Improve Your Church Parking Without Breaking the Bank", Unseminary.com

First begin with the outside of the property and take a close look at how people approach your building. Are there any potholes, broken, sunken or cracked sidewalks that could cause a trip and fall hazard? Does your signage clearly indicate how and where people are to park? Are entrances to certain parts of the building (i.e. gym, nursery, church office, etc.) clearly marked on the outside of the building and on signage indicating where to turn to find those assets? Is the writing on your signage legible and large enough to be read from a distance? Do trees and shrubbery need to be trimmed back so that signage is more easily read? How many parking spaces are designated as marked handicapped spots, and can more be added? Do all steps and ramps have handrails on both sides that go all the way to the bottom? A couple of ideas to consider include painting the curbs a different color so that there is better visual distinction between the sidewalk and the parking lot (Red signals a fire zone and no parking; yellow indicates a loading/unloading zone; blue can be a neutral color) and adding either reflective tape or non-skid tape to the edges of steps to make a better visual distinction.

Then look at how people gain entry to the building. How many points of access are there for those who use wheelchairs, walkers, and other mobility aids? Do those access points have doors that use a motion sensor or come with a handicapped button to automatically open the door? How hard to open are the doors? Do they need adjustment for a longer closing allowing those who walk slowly enough time to get through the door? If your building requires a doorbell to gain entry during weekday hours, is there a sign indicating the location of the doorbell and regular business hours? Is an emergency number listed?

Once inside the building, look at how people navigate inside. Is there signage at each entry point that indicates where certain places like restrooms, nursery, classrooms and worship centers are located? Is it possible to add pictographs to the signage (such as a toilet next to the word restroom, a baby next to the word nursery, etc.), as well as Braille, to accommodate those with cognitive problems, non-English speakers, and the blind? How easy to find are the restrooms? Do they have signage on the doors that include pictographs, and if they are in a recessed area, are there signs that stick out from the wall? Are there signs indicating other parts of the building that also include pictographs and Braille?

Part 2: Finding Solutions

UNIVERSAL SYMBOLS

Symbols can make navigating spaces easier for a wide range of different abilities. Consider these:

Restroom   Nursery   Stairs   Kitchen   Classroom   Elevator   Fire Extinguisher

Then look for trip and fall hazards. Decorative throw rugs should be eliminated throughout the building. Are there thresholds at doorways and between different flooring surfaces that can be lowered, eliminated or made more visible? Do long hallways have handrails? Are there slippery flooring surfaces that can be covered with a different surface? Are there floor signs, stanchions, furniture or other things that stick out into walking areas? Do interior steps and ramps have handrails on both sides that go all the way to the bottom? Can the edges of steps have a contrasting color to make better visual distinctions? Do hallways and rooms need brighter lighting? If there is a lot of walking required within the building, can a wheelchair be posted near entrances for people to borrow, and can benches be placed periodically so that someone can sit and rest?

> When Peace Lutheran Church outgrew its 1901 building, members could have cut costs substantially by using a smaller footprint and building two floors. Instead, the congregation in South Haven, Michigan, chose to design the whole church on a single level. Why? They wanted to make the entire worship space accessible so they asked for ideas from a church family that included a wheelchair user. "That commitment was unwavering as we sought to intersect with the whole South Haven area community," says Rev. Robert "Bob" Linstrom. The old church had pews but the new sanctuary uses chairs that can be easily moved to fit wheelchairs anywhere into a row of seats. The aisles and chancel are spacious, and a ramp accesses the chancel from behind the worship furnishings. "Wheelchairs are an occasional presence, but we have a number of members with walkers, canes, and the like who would be functionally homebound if we were still worshiping in our old facility. New members find our space welcoming. One new family has a child with spina bifida, who uses a wheelchair or special walker," Linstrom says. Joan Huyser-Honig, 2006. "Robert Nickola

Environmental Redesign

on Designing Equal Access Churches", Calvin Institute on Christian Worship,

Next look at the accessibility of each room. Do the doors have knobs or levered handles? How difficult to open are the doors? Do furniture pieces in each room have 36" of space between them to accommodate walkers and wheelchairs? Are there chairs with arms to make getting up and down easier? If chairs have wheels, can they be removed? Do some pews need to be removed to make seating more accessible for wheelchairs and walkers? Do the restrooms have at least one wheelchair-accessible stall, and do stall doors swing out instead of in? Are there grab bars and taller toilets in every stall? Do restrooms have at least one lowered sink or sinks within easy reach, and are soap and paper towel dispensers within easy reach?

Swing-clear hinges add extra width to doorways

During the environmental design audit, keep the Universal Design principles in mind while making a punch list of issues that should be repaired or modified. Also consider asking certain members such as older adults and those with disabilities to assist in the audit and get their feedback on what changes would be most effective. Discuss with your leadership and appropriate committees what changes need to be made, categorize them into tasks that can be easily completed and ones which need more planning, and identify members such as contractors or handypeople who could

Part 2: Finding Solutions

help facilitate changes. Chapters 19 and 20 discuss in more detail how to survey your congregation, which can help your leadership prioritize areas of concern.

Taking the time to assess the building's design means looking at it through another person's eyes. Think about times when you've stepped into buildings that were unfamiliar and confusing; did it make you feel welcome, or did it cause you frustration and anxiety? Sometimes older adults leave the church simply because it has become too difficult for them to navigate. Most of the changes that make the building more accommodating are fairly simple and cost-effective to put into place, but to someone who struggles with the challenges outlined in Part 1, those changes can make all the difference in the world.

10

Dementia-Friendly Faith Communities

As outlined in Chapter 2, dementia is already a crisis and getting worse year by year, so it is imperative that we as a nation learn how to accommodate ourselves to their unique needs. Faith communities all over the country are seeing the issues that dementia causes, such as decline in attendance as those with dementia and their caregivers can no longer attend services. However, another issue is how to advise those members who turn to the faith community for advice and help in times of crisis, when the leadership is unaware of what help might be available.

The first step in transitioning to a dementia-friendly church, synagogue or other place of worship is understanding dementia itself. It is caused by very complex and progressive disease processes and while some symptoms are common to each disease, everyone can experience dementia in their own way. That means that educating both members and leaders is essential. There are a variety of programs through which faith communities can gain a better understanding of dementia:

1. The Alzheimer's Association has community educators who are trained to present on several topics, such as the 10 Warning Signs of Alzheimer's, 10 Ways to Love Your Brain, Effective Communication Techniques, as well as deeper-dive topics on the financial implications of dementia, research, and more. These training sessions are free and available by contacting your local Alzheimer's Association chapter via Alz.org

Part 2: Finding Solutions

2. ALTER is a program specially designed to educate and support churches in communities of color, who experience dementia at twice the rate as their Caucasian counterparts. Churches that contact the ALTER program first receive a consultation, then receive a toolbox, ongoing support, education, and access to resources at no cost so that they are equipped to support families living with dementia. Their website is AlterDementia.com

3. Dementia Friendly America has free sector guides for faith communities that include an introductory video and tips for making your church a welcoming place. Go to DFAmerica.org > Resources > Sector Guides. Dementia Friendly Massachusetts also has an expanded sector guide for faith communities that includes a checklist, resource list, and articles. It is available at DFMassachusetts.org > Resources > Sector Guides.

4. Dementia Friends USA is another free educational resource. Anyone can go to the website, click a button that says "Become A Dementia Friend Today!", and be led through a series of short training videos, one of which is specific to faith communities. Some states may also be able to provide in-person training. Their website is DementiaFriendsUSA.org

5. Your local Area Agency on Aging and Disability may also have information about dementia educators in your area. You can find their contact information through the National Eldercare Locator, found at Eldercare.ACL.gov

6. There are several books available which are listed in the Resources section. Titles include: *Dementia-Friendly Worship, Ministry with the Forgotten: Dementia through a Spiritual Lens, No Act of Love is Ever Wasted: The Spirituality of Caring for Persons with Dementia, Reclaiming Joy Together: Building a Volunteer Community of Real Hope for Those with Dementia, Seasons of Caring: Meditations for Alzheimer's and Dementia Caregivers,* and *Spiritual Care for People Living with Dementia Using Multisensory Interventions*

The next step in creating a dementia-friendly place of worship is to audit the environment of the building, but through a dementia lens. Many of the modifications mentioned in the previous chapter have great benefits for those with dementia, but this time look for spaces that could be potentially hazardous such as the kitchen, cleaning closets, boiler rooms, etc. It can be helpful to place a red STOP sign on the door that says Authorized Personnel Only underneath. Be sure to keep the doors to cleaning closets, electrical rooms, boiler rooms, etc. locked at all times. Consider covering some doors to the outside with self-adhesive window coverings that are opaque or resemble stained glass to prevent wandering outside. Assess classroom and worship spaces for sensory overload. People with dementia often have a difficult time processing sensory input, so make sure there is minimized background noise, no flashing lights, etc. Some churches that have contemporary-style worship services use colored lighting and visual displays to enhance the worship experience; however, these may be too overstimulating or even scary for a person with cognitive challenges. Is there a room near the worship center that could be used as a sensory-friendly room where the service could be viewed on a tv screen?

Image from CreativeArtCo.com. A disguised door can prevent wandering

Next take a look at your programming to see whether or not it is inclusive for those with dementia, and what offerings could be modified or added. A couple of ideas to consider for inclusive programming include a dementia-friendly study of sacred texts class and a Memory Café.

1. A dementia- friendly sacred text study class could take place during the week or during Sunday School and utilize familiar stories and passages and familiar hymns and songs. Ideally it should be led by

someone who has had dementia training, have a volunteer to help keep participants engaged and refocused on the task at hand, and utilize handouts with large print and pictures. Participants who still have the ability to read should be encouraged to read short passages aloud, and facilitators should allow for conversations about the passage and memories of the songs. If you need some ideas to get started, check out the Spiritual Eldercare channel on YouTube for pre-recorded messages, scriptures and hymns.

2. A Memory Café is a time for those with dementia and their caregivers to come together for socialization and peer support. Memory Cafes are typically volunteer-led and may include snacks, music, activities, reminiscing, art, etc. They are also a great place to connect participants to education and community resources. They are not a drop-off or respite service, but rather a time for both those with dementia and their caregivers to come together to create moments of joy and connection with each other. For more information about what a Memory Café is (and isn't), where to locate existing ones in your area, and how to start your own, visit Dementia Friendly America at DFAmerica.org > Memory Café Alliance.

> "Having faith is very important to many people, including people with dementia. However, due to the difficulties caused by the condition, it can be hard for them to practice their faith as they previously did. By showing understanding, offering support and making small changes to the place and practice of worship, you might help someone with dementia to continue attending services or participate in faith-related activities in a way that is meaningful to them." Dr. Trevor Adams and Alli Anthony, "Developing a Dementia-Friendly Church: A Practical Guide Alzheimer's Society". Alzheimers.org.uk

The United Methodist Church Discipleship Ministries published a very useful article in 2015 that highlighted ways faith communities can be more dementia friendly. The article included a handy checklist[1]:

1. Are all areas of the church clutter-free, well lit, and mapped out or marked where they lead? Are there adequate storage places available

---

1. See The United Methodist Church Discipleship Ministries, "The Dementia-Friendly Church"

for unused items? Is there a process for checking to make sure items are put away when they are not in use in public areas?

2. Are classrooms free of complicated and misleading stimuli? Have you minimized background noise (radio, TV, computer, overhead speakers)?

3. What are the expectations of caregivers when church members visit their family member who has dementia? Are caregivers' needs being met with support groups? Are respite programs available? What strategies have been developed to deal with behavioral difficulties of those with dementia?

4. Have you simplified tasks and directions so that everyone, including people with dementia, can follow them?

5. In what ways is the church engaging people with dementia to prevent boredom, depression, and agitation while they are present? In what ways are church programs helping members with dementia experience service to others, purpose, joy, and hope? How can the skills and abilities of those with dementia be best used during their time at church to give them a sense of being normal?

6. What activities does the church offer that help to maintain the current cognitive function and spirituality of members with dementia? What new activities could a church offer, such as art therapy or dementia-oriented worship, which could be a family event?

7. What role can the church play in preserving the history and relationship of people with dementia with other members of the church? (For example, recording their memories before they are lost.) What opportunities exist to help those with dementia continue to express who they have been in life? Do activity designs allow people to be remembered for who they are, and not for their illness?

8. What is a church's "Plan B" for ministering to members with dementia and caregivers when they are no longer able to continue to participate in church activities? How will the church continue to minister effectively to, for, and with members when they become homebound or move to a skilled medical center?

9. Have you completed educational programs and training for leaders about dementia? Have you taken into consideration the needs of church members with dementia and their caregivers?

Part 2: Finding Solutions

10. Has a careful study of the building and grounds been undertaken? Have the following areas been checked?

    1. Restrooms: Have you set the hot water heater temperatures at 100°F or lower? Have you installed grab bars? Have you added textured stickers to slippery surfaces? Have you removed the locks from the bathroom doors?

    2. Kitchen: Is there a designated area for storage of cleaning supplies that is kept locked? Can electricity be turned off to the garbage disposal and any appliances when not in use? Are knives and other utensils stored in locked areas? Can appliances such as toasters, microwaves, and blenders be locked up or turned off? Can gas service to gas appliances be switched off when not in use? Or can the stove be connected to a hidden gas valve or electric switch, so it is impossible for it to accidentally be turned on? Is there a fire extinguisher nearby? Are the refrigerators cleaned out regularly?

    3. Storage areas: Is there a plan to ensure that doors to storage areas are locked from the outside? Are tools such as drills, axes, saws, and picks locked up? Is there only limited access to large equipment, such as lawn equipment? Are all poisonous chemicals, such as paint and cleaners, locked up?

    4. Throughout the church: Have you disguised doors or set door alarms to the outside to prevent people with dementia from wandering? Have you removed or taped down throw rugs? Have colored stickers been applied to large windows and sliding glass doors? Have you removed poisonous plants or other items that might accidentally get eaten? Is there sufficient lighting near doorways, stairways, and between rooms? Have you removed objects that block walking paths?

    7 Guiding Principles for Dementia-Friendly Faith Communities

    1. Adopt a positive attitude. Just because someone has dementia does not mean they cannot hear what is being said around them, or cannot participate in conversation or activities. Things might just need doing a bit differently.

2. Encourage supportive relationships. People with dementia may not always remember what was said to them, but may remember how you made them feel.
3. Facilitate communication. People with dementia may struggle with spoken language, yet they can often still read and use body language to express themselves.
4. Create an accessible environment. Small, inexpensive changes to the physical environment can help a person with dementia find their way around and feel more comfortable and at ease.
5. Encourage creativity. All people, including those with dementia, thrive and flourish when they are given the opportunity to be creative.
6. Part of a larger network. Dementia-friendly churches exist within a wider network of people, agencies and organizations that contribute towards the well-being of people with dementia.
7. Learn from others. By supporting people with dementia to express their faith, we can in turn all learn to better express our own.

Dr. Trevor Adams and Alli Anthony, "Developing a Dementia-Friendly Church: A Practical Guide". Alzheimer's Society. Alzheimers.org.uk

The article went on to include A Dozen Quick Ideas to Become a More Dementia-Friendly Church. The articles mentioned in the tips are included in the bibliography of this book for your convenience.

1. Host Alzheimer's and dementia caregiver's support group meetings. (Group leader training is available free through the Alzheimer's Association at Alz.org).
2. Offer a monthly respite time or day for caregivers of members with dementia. Include activities for those who have dementia besides sitting, sleeping, or watching television.
3. Help people with dementia and caregivers look good by sponsoring a quarterly makeover day with area volunteers and cosmetologists. (Cosmetology and barber schools are a great resource.)

PART 2: FINDING SOLUTIONS

4. Offer a weekly or monthly special worship service for members with dementia or designate special Dementia Sundays where the main worship service is designed specifically for those with dementia. Include familiar hymns rather than new ones in the service. (Resources are available from the Office on Aging and Older-Adult Ministry.)

5. Look for talents and abilities in people with dementia that they can develop and share with other people in the church. Affirm them in performing their service by acknowledging and thanking them before the entire church.

6. Train church leaders and members in dementia awareness and strategies for dealing with potential challenges that might arise.

7. Offer a Memory Café where the memory-impaired and their caregivers can gather to remember. Consider a workshop on making memory boxes for members with dementia and their caregivers.

8. Have leaders of the church agree to and sign a code of behavior for interacting with members with dementia. (Examples of this would be listening patiently when members with dementia tell the same story over and over again; listening to what people with dementia are saying; avoiding correcting people with dementia when they do something improperly.)

9. Offer a resource or reading center on dementia as well as a dementia newsletter with a review of some of the latest news on Alzheimer's. (This information can be obtained by joining US Against Alzheimer's and signing up for daily updates.)

10. Develop a visitation team to visit members with dementia when they become homebound or move to a skilled medical center. Include regular Communion deliveries and videos of worship services in the visits.

11. Research, develop, and print a community resource guide for caregivers of those who have dementia.

12. Develop a daily or weekly prayer chain and checking-in program for the families and caregivers of those who have dementia to minister to their mental, emotional, and spiritual well-being.

For additional information on dementia-friendly worship, please reference the Resources section of this book for materials available through Clergy Against Alzheimer's.

Dementia-Friendly Faith Communities

Becoming a dementia-friendly place of worship is a process that can take time, however, your faith community can at least take steps now to improve communication techniques with those who have dementia. Here are 10 Tips for Better Communication provided by Memory Makers of the Midsouth:

1. Get on eye level and limit distractions. People with dementia have a shorter attention span and a harder time filtering out background noises, movement, and lights. Move to a quieter space or turn off tv, radio, etc. to help them focus.

2. Speak slowly & allow more time for a response. People with dementia have a harder time processing speech, so speak more slowly and give them extra time to respond.

3. Only ask one question at a time. Because they have a harder time processing information, only ask one question at a time. You may need to ask the question more than once or restate it in a different way.

4. Only give two choices at a time. It is easier for a person with dementia to decide between two things than to ask an open-ended question, like "what do you want to eat?"

5. Watch your body language and tone of voice. Making your body language and tone of voice match what you are trying to convey can help them understand better.

6. Explain what you are doing as you are doing it. If you are helping a person with dementia with a care task, or moving their wheelchair, explain what you are doing and why, so they don't misinterpret your actions.

7. Talk to them, not about them. Always include them in your conversation instead of talking about them as if they aren't there.

8. Use aids such as whiteboards and clocks. A person with dementia usually has trouble with short-term memory; use whiteboards, signs, and clocks to remind them.

9. Respond to the emotion, not the words or actions. A person with dementia may act out or become fearful or agitated. *Behind every behavior is an emotion, and behind every emotion is an unmet need.*

10. Find ways to laugh. Humor can go a long way towards defusing tense situations. Just don't use negative humor, sarcasm, or make fun of someone.

Part 2: Finding Solutions

While the lists and tips in this chapter may seem overwhelming, focus on what your place of worship can feasibly accomplish and ask those members caring for a person with dementia what would be the most helpful. Transitioning to a dementia-friendly faith community is a process that can take some time and buy-in from leadership and members. First dementia has to be recognized as an issue in your particular place of worship; if it is something that is not already on the radar screen, perhaps there is a lack of awareness, and the subject can be introduced softly with an educational seminar. If it has already been recognized as a significant issue, then it is a matter of developing a plan to address it that uses the suggestions outlined in this chapter. It is important to note that members who have dementia are still valued members who deserve spiritual support. It is wrong to assume that a person with cognitive problems doesn't understand what is going on; in many cases they can be very aware of their surroundings and can find much comfort in being in a familiar environment with scriptures, songs, and stories that they've heard many times over and turned to for strength and hope over the years. Furthermore, being in an environment that is safe, welcoming, understanding, and adapted to fit their needs helps a person with dementia feel as if he or she is not alone and that their faith community has not abandoned them in their illness.

Why Faith Communities Should Engage With People With Dementia.

1. People with dementia are loved by God. They need to be treated with respect and dignity, as well as receiving support to maintain the outward expression of their faith.
2. People with dementia reflect God's image. This means that every person, whatever their mental abilities, displays in part what God is like.
3. People with dementia have much to contribute. Without people living with dementia, the Church is incomplete and cannot gain from everyone's experiences.

"The person travelling down the dementia road is no less valued or loved by God, . . . it is our extrinsic relationships with other persons that confer on us our identity as a 'self', and it is the loving relationship that God maintains with us that constitutes the . . . image of God."- John & Susan McFadden. Dr. Trevor Adams and Alli Anthony, "Developing a Dementia-Friendly Church: A Practical Guide". Alzheimer's Society. Alzheimers.org.uk

11

Communication Redesign

Chapter 3 explored the challenge of vision and hearing loss, so this chapter will look at solutions to accommodate those challenges for your older adult members, which in turn can make your place of worship more accessible for others with disabilities. This chapter will explore not only print, auditory, and digital media, but also how to move away from ageist and ableist language and behaviors.

Before jumping into tips on things like formatting and fonts, it is important to first understand how to communicate with those who have varying degrees of ability by being mindful of how they would prefer to be treated and to how they should be referred. You may have noticed that this book does not routinely use words like "senior", "elders", or "old people" to describe those who are in older adulthood; these terms are considered ageist because they imply that older adults are frail, sickly, or burdensome, which is clearly not the case across the board. Also, those terms can be confusing; at what age does one become a "senior" or "old"? The same is true for people with disabilities. Rather than saying "a blind person" or "a wheelchair-bound person" which implies that someone is defined by their medical condition, the more appropriate description would be "person who is blind" or "person who uses a wheelchair". This is called Person First Language. Other terms to avoid when referring to people include handicapped, disabled, vision/hearing impaired, autistic, dementia patient, dwarf/midget, invalid, crippled, etc. Remember everyone is a person first and a diagnosis second. Bridging the Gap Project has a helpful chart of what language is preferable to use.

In addition to being mindful of language, faith community leaders and members should also be mindful of their behavior when encountering a person with disabilities. Bridging the Gap Project[1] recommends:

1. Address people with disabilities in the same way as you talk to everyone else; speak directly to them, even if there is an interpreter.

2. Use a normal tone of voice; don't patronize, shout, or talk down.

3. Ask first when aiding a person with disabilities, wait until your offer is accepted before you help and then follow the instructions of the person.

4. Be patient to get things done or said. Let the person set the pace in talking and doing things. [This is especially important for those who have dementia]

5. It is appropriate to use the usual cultural greeting, i.e., shaking hands for example, when introducing to a person with disabilities, as well as in the case of people with limited hand use or who wear an artificial limb.

6. To get the attention of a person who is deaf or hard of hearing, wave your hand or tap on the person's shoulder when culturally appropriate.

7. Look directly at the person and speak clearly, slowly and expressively without overreacting/overemoting to establish if the person can read your lips.

8. Keep your hands and food away from your mouth when speaking. Avoid communicating while smoking or chewing gum.

9. If you have trouble understanding the speech of a person who is deaf or hard of hearing, let him/her know

10. Written notes can often facilitate communication.

11. When communicating with a person who is blind or partially sighted, always identify yourself and others who may be with you.

12. Indicate when you move from one place to another and if you leave or return to a room.

---

1. See Bridging the Gap, "Inclusive and Accessible Communication"

13. When you offer to assist someone with vision loss, allow the person to take your arm to better guide this person.
14. When offering seating, place the person's hand on the back or arm of the seat
15. Give whole, unhurried attention when talking to a person who has difficulty speaking.
16. Allow extra time for communication.
17. Keep your manner encouraging rather than correcting. Be patient, do not speak for the person.
18. If a person has an intellectual disability or problems with cognition, be patient. Take the time necessary to ensure clear understanding and give them time to put thoughts into words, especially when responding to a question.
19. Formulate simple sentences and repeat as necessary. You may need to describe what you're saying in a different way.
20. Do not give too many directions at one time.
21. When speaking with someone in a wheelchair, talk directly to the person and try to be at his/her eye level, but do not kneel. If you must stand, step back slightly so the person doesn't have to strain his/her neck to see you.
22. When giving directions to people with mobility limitations, consider distance, weather conditions and physical obstacles such as stairs, curbs and steep hills.
23. Always ask before you move a person in a wheelchair.
24. If a person transfers from a wheelchair to a car, toilet, etc., leave the wheelchair within easy reach. Always make sure that a wheelchair or rollator (walker with wheels) is locked before helping a person transfer.
25. Service animals, such as guide dogs for blind people are working animals, not pets. They should not be petted or otherwise distracted when in harness.

Part 2: Finding Solutions

> Pitfalls of Social Security Disability. Because the Social Security Act defines disability so strictly, Social Security disability beneficiaries are among the most severely impaired in the country. In fact, Social Security disability beneficiaries are more than three times as likely to die in a year as other people the same age. Among those who start receiving disability benefits at the age of 55, 1-in-6 men and 1-in-8 women die within five years of the onset of their disabilities.
>
> At the beginning of 2019, Social Security paid an average monthly disability benefit of about $1,234 to all disabled workers. That is barely enough to keep a beneficiary above the 2018 poverty level ($12,140 annually). SSA.gov. "The Faces and Facts of Disability".

According to the Americans with Disabilities Act, Title III entities (businesses and nonprofits that serve the general public) are required to "ensure that communication with people with these disabilities is equally effective as communication with people without disabilities."[2] Effective Communication includes auxiliary aids and services, such as assisted listening devices, screen readers, interpreters, and companions, but does allow limitations for undue burdens of cost or fundamentally altering the nature of services provided to the public. What that means for faith communities is that they should take what measures they are able to incorporate effective communication.

One easy way to start is to look at your bulletins, newsletters, flyers, emails, and other printed materials. Here are a few tips from the Bridging the Gap Project to make your print work easier to read for those who have problems with vision:

1. Matte white or pale-yellow paper are preferable to glossy and darker paper
2. Century Gothic and Arial fonts that are at least 16 points are easier to see
3. The color contrast of typeface to background—either dark on light or light on dark—should be high. A 70% contrast is recommended.
4. Avoid using italics and splitting words with a hyphen (such as at the end of a line)

2. See U.S. Dept. of Justice Civil Right Division, "Effective Communication"

Communication Redesign

5. Instead of having words center-aligned, align words to the left
6. Rather than use columns, use bullet points instead
7. Do not place any type or illustrations, such as watermarks, over other designs, photographs, graphics or text.
8. Use shorter sentences and easier-to-understand language
9. Show contact information with address, phone number, email address and website rather than just relying on a QR code
10. Emphasize words using bold, instead of capital letters or underlining

> There are varying degrees of visual impairment, which can be described differently according to the World Health Organization. Low vision: Someone has visual clarity between 20/70 to 20/400 or a visual field of 20 degrees or less, even with correction. Blindness: Someone has visual acuity worse than 20/400 or a visual field of 10 degrees or less, even with correction. If you have 20/70 visual acuity, you can only see what a person with normal vision sees at 70 feet when standing 20 feet away. But if you have 20/400, you can only see what a normal-sighted person sees at 400 feet when standing at the same distance of 20 feet. Alyssa Hill, 2024. "Visual Impairment Accessibility". VisionCenter.org.

Next, review how well members can hear the service. Not every place of worship is required to have Assisted Listening Technology under the Americans with Disabilities Act, but some states make it provisional to be in compliance. Personal listening devices have been in worship services for years, but some of the technology has improved and changed in both the listening devices as well as in hearing aids. According to an article from Church Tech Today, "Wireless assisted listening systems are available in a variety of formats. The three primary wireless technologies used are: RF (radio frequency), IR (infrared), and Loop (induction loop). RF systems are great for wireless coverage of a large area. Transmitters and receivers can use a variety of frequencies ranging from FM to Wifi bands. The most common wireless frequencies are in the 72 MHz and 216 MHz bands. [RF systems can work for users that use telecoil-compatible hearing aids as well as cochlear implants.] IR systems are perfect for rooms that have heavy wireless frequency interference or require privacy. Since IR transmits signals using invisible infrared light (like a TV remote control), it only works in line-of-sight environments. Induction loop systems work well for users that use telecoil-compatible hearing aids. A wired loop is carefully installed

Part 2: Finding Solutions

around the perimeter of a room or facility and anyone with a compatible hearing aid will automatically receive the assisted listening system signal when they enter the induction loop coverage zone."[3] All of these systems have their own pros, cons, and costs to be considered, but they all come with signage letting members know that the technology is available. Another option to consider is personal sound amplifiers which members can borrow at the beginning of the service and return at the end of the service.

> What is a Telecoil? A telecoil, also called a t-coil, is a coil of wire that is installed inside many hearing aids and cochlear implants to act as a miniature wireless receiver. It was originally designed to make sounds clearer to a listener over the telephone. It also is used with a variety of other assistive listening devices, such as hearing loop (or induction loop) systems, FM systems, infrared systems, and personal amplifiers. Many cochlear implants have a telecoil built into the sound processor, or can use an external telecoil accessory with both hearing aid compatible telephones and public loop systems. A simple switch or programming maneuver performed by the user activates this function. National Institute on Deafness and Other Communication Disorders, "Assistive Devices for People with Hearing, Voice, Speech, or Language Disorders". NIDCD.NIH.gov

This logo informs people that a public area is looped.

3. See Church Tech Today, "Assisted Listening Systems"

Communication Redesign

Finally, review your digital media including website and PowerPoint presentations. How easy is it for people viewing your website to navigate and find the information they need? Here are a few tips from the Bridging The Gap Project on making your website more accessible:

1. Use clear navigation structure throughout the site, including the main navigation buttons at the top and at the bottom of the page
2. Each page should indicate the place where the user is clearly and showing the navigation menu of the site.
3. Select colors with high contrast to facilitate reading. The tool ContrastChecker.com is a good help for choosing the colors.
4. Backgrounds should be simple with high contrast to text and graphics.
5. Avoid using numerous graphic images, which should all have an alternative text explaining the content (for those who use screen readers).
6. E-mail or telephone contacts should be provided as alternatives to web forms.

   Web Content Accessibility Guidelines.
   1. Perceivable: Website visitors should be able to perceive website content and information through various senses.
   2. Operable: Website visitors need to be able to operate your website regardless of ability. Visitors should be able to navigate the site using different methods like a keyboard or assistive technologies, regardless of their physical condition.
   3. Understandable: Website visitors should be able to easily understand content and instructions without confusion.
   4. Robust: For your website to be robust, it needs to use HTML and CSS according to specification, and be compatible with assistive technologies and devices like screen readers.

   AccessiBe.com, "Twenty Examples of Stunning Accessible Websites". June 25, 2024

If you use PowerPoint presentations to enhance your worship experience, teach classes, or facilitate meetings, some best practices include:

1. Present only one idea per slide with a maximum of six bullet points.
2. Simplify the information using key words, not complete sentences

3. Use Century Gothic and Arial fonts as these are accessible, and at least a font size of 24 points.
4. Always justify text to the left.
5. Avoid large and/or complicated tables. If necessary, use simple graphics.
6. Ensure there is enough time for people to read each visual.

Making some small changes to the various forms of communication can make a huge difference to a person with hearing or vision loss, who often feels left out of the worship experience. Aside from the Assisted Listening Technology, all the other changes can be made at no cost and only require some mindfulness. It is highly recommended that faith community members and leaders who have challenges with vision and hearing be included in conversations about communication accessibility and asked what things they find helpful.

> What Types of Assistive Devices Are Available? Assistive listening devices (ALDs) help amplify the sounds you want to hear, especially when there's a lot of background noise. ALDs can be used with a hearing aid or cochlear implant to help a wearer hear certain sounds better.
>
> Augmentative and alternative communication (AAC) devices help people with communication disorders to express themselves. These devices can range from a simple picture board to a computer program that synthesizes speech from text. Alerting devices connect to a doorbell, telephone, or alarm that emits a loud sound or blinking light to let someone with hearing loss know that an event is taking place. National Institute on Deafness and Other Communication Disorders. NIDCD.NIH.gov

12

Inclusive Programming

ONE OF THE CHALLENGES that many faith communities face is the spectrum of life stages that encompass older age. At one end of the spectrum is the younger older adults who are recently retired or nearing retirement that are the most active. In the middle of the spectrum are those older adults who are still able to be active, but not quite as much as their younger counterparts. At the other end of the spectrum are those who are unable to be active and may be mostly homebound. So how then can a place of worship include programming to fit the entire spectrum that addresses the challenge of social isolation?

A 2016 article written by Ken Satterfield for *Word & Way* interviewed pastors about their thoughts on older adult ministries. Bill Baer, a pastoral care minister at Second Baptist Church in Springfield, Missouri was noted as saying, "Senior adults are not all alike... Some are still very active socially, physically and are very involved in various ministries. Others struggle with very serious health issues. Some have a life-long history of being active in church, and others are new to the church scene or are ambivalent about being involved in church. So senior adults, like any other age group, are very diverse."[4] Baer also noted challenges for consideration such as different approaches to sacred text study, new and different non-religious activities, older adults who are still working and have family obligations,

---

4. See Ken Satterfield, "Senior Adult Ministries"

health issues, widowhood vs. living with a spouse, etc. It stands to reason that a one-size-fits-all method of programming for older adults is far less effective than including programs for adults across the older age spectrum. Rabbi Micah Greenstein from Temple Israel in Memphis, Tennessee also noted in a survey for this book that, "I have found that older members are as diverse as younger members, so we offer an array of programs, from music and study to prayer and game nights. However, what seems to work best is simply weekly "Coffee and Conversation". This chapter will explore unique religious and non-religious programming suggestions for active older adults, mid-stage older adults, and homebound older adults, as well as suggestions on how those three groups can help each other.

When looking at active older adult programs, the date and time of the program offering is just as important as the program itself. This group may still be working or caring for grandchildren and may be more able to participate in activities in the evening and on weekends, but perhaps on a monthly basis rather than a weekly basis. They may also be more interested in social activities such as hiking, walking or fitness classes; going out to eat at restaurants; attending museums and attractions; and overnight travel. Volunteering and short-term mission trip opportunities may also be very appealing to active older adults, and things for consideration could include a food/clothing/diaper bank for the community, Habitat for Humanity projects, Stephen Ministry, cleaning up after storm damage, Vacation Bible School volunteers, and other projects that require a certain amount of energy. Support groups for those caring for an older loved one or raising grandchildren; classes on marriage enrichment or retirement issues like finances, insurance, and dealing with loss of identity or purpose; and lunchtime sacred text studies via Zoom are all good possibilities for this group as well. Since the majority of active older adults likely still drive, they may be able to minister to other older adults by offering rides to the church or synagogue, store, or doctors' offices. Sacred text study topics that explore how older adults can continue to serve and make a difference may be of particular interest, since retirement can make one question their purpose in this stage of life. Rabbi Richard Address noted in an interview for this book that this stage of life calls for a more "mature spirituality"; older adults don't necessarily need to hear the same stories about heroes of the faith that they've heard all their lives but rather would prefer to discuss texts and passages related to loss, caregiving, and other relevant topics.

Inclusive Programming

Importance of Activities. "In the realm of senior wellness, the value of inclusive social activities for seniors cannot be overstated. These activities serve as a vital catalyst in promoting mental health and overall well-being among the elderly. Engaging seniors in diverse social activities is not just about filling their time; it's a crucial step towards fostering a sense of belonging and community. In recent years, a growing body of research has underscored the positive impact of social engagement on the elderly. Participating in community events and inclusive activities offers numerous benefits, including reduced risk of depression, improved cognitive functions, and a greater sense of fulfilment." Bhanupriya Rawat Kitt, 2024. "Inclusive Social Activities for Seniors: Engaging Solutions". ElderProofing.net

When looking at programs for those in the mid-stage of older adulthood, the time and date of those programs are critical as well. People in this group may have more health and mobility issues and may have stopped driving at night. They may be more likely to participate in activities during the weekday on a weekly basis, and because this group has a higher likelihood of being widowed, regular socialization is vitally important to maintaining independence and cognition. Social activities such as luncheons, learning seminars, and entertainment at the place of worship; bus outings to local restaurants; chair exercises; book clubs; art, music, or gardening classes; and game days may be more appealing for this group. Mid-stage older adults also make great volunteers and may enjoy opportunities such as reading to children; making flower arrangements for nursing homes; knitting, crocheting, or quilting items for the homeless; bagging food pantry items for distribution; and other useful things that don't require a lot of driving or heavy lifting. Support groups for grief or caring for a spouse; classes on health and wellness topics or living alone; and in-person sacred text studies can also be great possibilities. Mid-stage older adults can also minister to other older adults by making visits to nursing homes and those who are homebound, sending cards, making calls, and bringing meals to those recently returned from the hospital. Sacred text study topics that deal with life's changes can be encouraging, as can studying passages that deal with life challenges and adversities. Pastor Bob Turner from Church of Christ White Station in Memphis, Tennessee stated in a survey that, "Our city-facing programs throughout the week are the key ways that older members engage the community and connect with one another. We have a Community Exercise Class, coffee house, food pantry, clothes closet, sewing ministry, support groups, prayer gatherings, Bible studies, ministry to foster families, homeless ministry, and much more. Some older members don't drive at night, so having morning opportunities are huge."

> 7 Ways to Make Activities Inclusive
>
> 1. Assess interests first—Understand the senior's passions and tailor activities around their likes and dislikes for more engaging experiences.
> 2. Consider abilities—Choose activities that accommodate physical limitations or health issues. Adapt games by using lightweight equipment or shorter playing fields.
> 3. Contact organizers—Reach out to activity leaders in advance to discuss required accommodations and get insights on ensuring a senior-friendly environment.
> 4. Research accessibility—Check that venues have ramps, elevators and ample seating. Confirm wheelchair-accessible paths and transportation options.
> 5. Use assistive devices—Encourage using walking sticks, mobility scooters or other aids to enable full, comfortable participation.
> 6. Involve caregivers—Invite family members or friends to join activities to provide social interaction and any needed assistance.
> 7. Gather feedback—Monitor experiences and get input on enjoyment and suggested improvements to better cater to their preferences.
>
> Scott Grant, 2024. "29 Activities to Engage and Inspire Seniors This Summer". GrayingWithGrace.com

Programs that are inclusive for those who are homebound or living in a facility mean meeting them where they are, since they most likely have a lot of difficulty getting out to go to a place of worship. Visits, phone calls, cards, and letters go a long way towards making a person in this stage of life feel remembered and special; Beaver Baptist Church in Brighton, Tennessee says, "We have a team of servants who partner up once a week to prepare and deliver meals, we have visits in the homes of shut-ins each week, we help them access sermons and Bible studies at home, send them bulletins of the current events." They even go so far as to include children and

Inclusive Programming

youth: "The children's program takes vans to the homes of shut-ins to sing, the youth rake and clean their yards and homes." Homebound older adults can be included in sacred text study, Sunday School classes, prayer groups, and even worship services via speakerphone or FaceTime. For example, an older person or couple that can no longer get to church could be included in worship by having them read the scripture or pray via speakerphone. One unique idea could be a Vacation Bible School that takes place in a senior living facility that includes an hour or two for a Bible story, songs, and simple crafts. Another idea is for members of the choir to go and sing hymns at a facility. People in this group also need to feel useful and purposeful, and they can minister to others by making calls, serving as prayer warriors, knitting or crocheting, and sending cards, depending on their abilities. Sacred text study topics that focus on strengthening faith during times of crisis may bring comfort as they approach the end of their lives.

One thing to keep in mind when designing older adult programs is that the possibilities for programs can start to get overwhelming. One model that faith communities may find helpful is the SENIORS Ministry model, which stands for Spiritual, Enrichment, Nutrition, Intergenerational, Outreach, Recreation, and Service. Here are some basic guidelines for using the SENIORS Ministry model:[1]

1. Spiritual- encompasses activities such as worship, sacred text study, prayer groups, journaling sessions, and healing services.
2. Enrichment- encompasses activities that include opportunities for learning, like classes on financial topics, wellness, technology, the environment, travel, etc.
3. Nutrition- encompasses physical wellness activities such as meals, food pantries, exercise, and health education.
4. Intergenerational- encompasses activities that strengthen bonds between older and younger people in different stages of life
5. Outreach- encompasses activities that share faith to others at all stages of life, including older adults
6. Recreation- encompasses activities that promote fun, laughter, and socialization and can be anything from outings to picnics to fishing to board games and everything in between.

---

1. See Richard H. Gentzler, Jr., "S.E.N.I.O.R.S. Ministry"

Part 2: Finding Solutions

7. Service- encompasses activities that help people feel purposeful and useful by doing good for others.

Another model faith communities can use to develop inclusive older adult programs is the 8 Dimensions of Wellness from the Substance Abuse and Mental Health Services Administration. This model will be more fully explored later in this book.

However the older adult programs are designed, the activities contained within should be intentional, be designed with the assistance of the older adults themselves based on their needs and interests and incorporate a holistic approach that cares for the mind, body, and spirit. Some programs can also be both in-person and virtual hybrids to accommodate both working older adults and homebound older adults.

How else can faith communities have programs that are more inclusive for older members? One suggestion from Dorothy Linthicum in her 2016 article entitled, "Faith Formation After 70: Ministry with Older Adults" is for congregations to "celebrate [the mission and outreach initiatives that began with the efforts of people who are now over 75]—with more than just a line in a worship bulletin—the role the events played in the life of the church and the people who made them possible. The Builder Generation laid the foundation that allows the current congregation to change and grow"[2] Another suggestion included "A church service each year honoring senior adults and talking about their importance to the church is another way to make seniors feel important and that they belong"[3]

Having programs that fit the needs of the whole spectrum of older adulthood can not only disrupt the terrible cycle of social isolation and decline but can immensely benefit the health of the entire church by keeping older members engaged and active in ministry, service, and discipleship. Pastor Bob Turner at Church of Christ White Station said it well when he stated that, "I hope churches can recover a better language to think about this stage of life than "retirement." It's not a biblical word or idea. The most joyful people we have in that age group at White Station did not stop working; they just pivoted to a type of work that they weren't able to do during their career years. It's really beautiful—and a lot more rewarding than spending every day at the golf course or glued to cable news."

2. See Dorothy Linthicum, "Faith Formation After 70"

3. See The United Methodist Church Discipleship Ministries, "48 Older Adult Ministry Ideas"

Inclusive Programming

Homebound-Friendly Faith Communities. "In some churches, the homebound (who are primarily older adults and their caregivers) may be forgotten, ignored, or misunderstood. . .The homebound need to have fellowship brought to them. They miss their friends and the fellowship of other church members. . .Homebound-friendly churches understand disabilities and the aging process and how these affect the psychological, physical, and emotional states of those unable to participate in worship and the life of the church. Homebound-friendly churches address the whole person, including the need to feel purposeful and meaningfully involved with the church community. . . The homebound-friendly church recognizes the gifts of the homebound. There are a variety of ministries in which the homebound can participate from their homes."

UMCDiscipleship.org, "When Church Members Become Homebound". May 13, 2015

13

Caring for the Carers

THE CHALLENGES OF CAREGIVING outlined in chapter 5 of this book on caregiving present a unique opportunity for faith communities to be the "hands and feet" for those caregivers. In this chapter we will explore both traditional and non-traditional approaches to supporting the caregivers in your community for their three biggest needs- education, support, and respite.

Education for caregivers is probably the easiest solution to implement. Here are some ideas for your place of worship to explore:

1. Hosting a monthly lunch and learn (offering it both in-person and virtually for better accommodation) and providing speakers for topics such as safe lifting and transferring techniques; understanding dementia and better communication techniques; skin integrity; nutrition and exercise; fall prevention; stress management; options for care; and other relevant topics is a great place to start. Speakers can be local nurses, physical therapists, counselors, dementia educators, etc.

2. A Caregiver Resource Fair where attendees can browse local vendors to get relevant information can also be a great idea. Invite those who work in the senior services industry, which encompasses businesses such as senior living communities, home care, hospice and palliative care, insurance, local Area Agency on Aging, health department, transportation providers, and more. Perhaps your church could host

an annual Caregiver Conference that includes educational speakers as well as vendors.

3. There is also a formal, evidence-based caregiver training program called Powerful Tools for Caregivers. If someone in your church is willing to be trained as a facilitator, they can take the training and receive materials to teach the 6-week long course both in-person and virtually. Or perhaps your church could offer a classroom space so that attendees can join in a program offered elsewhere virtually.

4. Another option is to help caregivers connect to other education programs via the Best Practice Caregiving directory. Both the directory and Powerful Tools for Caregivers are listed in the Resources section of this book.

> "Very few other social institutions are as well placed to face the challenges of providing care for caregivers as the church." CollegevilleInstitute.org

Support groups and pastoral counseling can also help caregivers process the myriads of emotions that come with providing care for another person. Stephen Ministers can walk alongside caregivers for emotional and spiritual support and encouragement. If someone in your place of worship is willing and able to facilitate a support group, that is a wonderful place to start as well. However, your faith institution can still serve the community by offering a classroom space for support groups from the Alzheimer's Association, Parkinson's Foundation, American Cancer Society, and others. Just having a local space can go a long way toward reaching out to caregivers in your community, whether or not they attend your worship services.

> Caregiving is often a long-term calling, and the challenges continue long after the church's initial burst of enthusiastic help. "A family in a long-term caregiving situation needs more than just people cheering them on at the beginning of the journey. . .Just like an ultra-marathon runner, we need stops for water and Gatorade along the way. We need people with cowbells at random spots along the road cheering us on and reminding us they are on our side. This is a long, exhausting journey. Don't forget us." Simonetta Carr, 2024. "How to Support the Caregivers in Your Church", Ligionier.org

Part 2: Finding Solutions

Respite means having a rest or temporary relief from burdens and many faith communities across the country are developing Respite Ministries. Respite ministries take on the act of caregiving in order to give family caregivers a much-needed break from duties so that they can go to doctors' appointments, go shopping, and perform other household and self-care tasks.

There are a couple of different ways to implement a respite ministry. The first way is to have a group of trained respite volunteers who can go in pairs to a person's house and provide companionship for their loved one for a short while. Going in pairs ensures the safety of the volunteers as well as a reduction in liability since the person they are there to visit is a vulnerable adult due to physical frailty or cognitive issues. The benefits of this type of respite ministry are that it can require fewer volunteers, is flexible on time and date, and does not take place on the church or synagogue grounds; it also benefits caregivers who may not be able to afford professional caregiving services or only need respite care occasionally. When considering this type of respite ministry, it is important for your leadership and volunteers to have written protocols in place. Some things to consider might include:

1. Which days of the week will this service be available?
2. How many hours per session are feasible?
3. What are the risks involved?
4. If the care receiver has an emergency while the respite volunteers are there, what are the procedures?
5. What tasks are reasonable for a volunteer to do while providing respite?
6. How will volunteers be trained?
7. What are the limits on how often a family caregiver can utilize the respite ministry?
8. What are the protocols if a volunteer suspects abuse or neglect?
9. What will the policies be in reference to families who have pets or who smoke in the house?
10. What are the protocols if the family caregiver fails to return home at the appointed time?
11. What will the policies be if the care receiver has incontinence and needs to be changed while the volunteers are there?

12. What are the expectations of the family caregiver?
13. What safety concerns does the family caregiver need to share with volunteers?

A good best practice for implementing in-home respite ministry could be the leadership and volunteer team visiting with the potential care receiver and family caregiver beforehand and discussing the policies of the program so that expectations can be met, and risks can be minimized.

> Please Understand. "Trina, who spent years caring for her husband during his struggle with dementia and cancer, has sad memories of people limiting their prayers to the healing of cancer, while both she and her husband thought God had allowed it as a merciful end to his rapid mental decline. No one prayed for her and their children with her present. "We needed endurance and had concerns about pain relief, end of life decisions, and other issues," she said. "People need to listen to or read the prayer requests and pray for those things, particularly in the hearing of the patient and caregiver. We need to feel heard by those we look to for support. And their prayers must support reality, not the wishes of the one praying."
>
> Simonetta Carr, 2024. "How to Support the Caregivers in Your Church" Ligionier.org

The second type of respite ministry is a day program hosted by the place of worship. This type of respite is more appropriate for those with dementia and works well for areas that are lacking in adult day programs because it allows the participants to get much-needed socialization. Day programs offer more stability on date and time offerings, as well as expectations of what tasks and activities can feasibly be offered. They are normally run by a dedicated team of trained volunteers and overseen by a church staff member who acts as the program director. When considering this type of respite ministry, it is important for your leadership and volunteers to have written protocols in place. Some things to consider might include:

1. What days and times will the respite ministry take place?
2. Which rooms in the church building will be utilized, and how close are they to restrooms?
3. What activities will take place and what will the daily schedule be?

Part 2: Finding Solutions

4. Will there be meals and snacks offered?
5. What is the cost of running this type of ministry?
6. Are there grants available to implement this program?
7. Will there be a daily fee for participants, or will the program be offered for free?
8. What are the protocols for handling emergencies and incontinence accidents?
9. Would a day program be covered by the church's liability insurance?
10. How will volunteers be trained?
11. What is the job description for the person directing the program?
12. What abilities would participants need to have in order to participate?
13. Would this program be open to the community or only congregation members?

There is much more literature available on faith institution-based day respite programs that answer these questions and many others. Two good sources of information are *Walking With Grace: Tools For Implementing And Launching A Congregational Respite Program* by Robin Dill which is available on Amazon.com, and RespiteForAll.com which includes a full training roadmap. Both sources are listed in the Resources section of this book. Both types of respite ministry offer much value to the care recipients, their family caregivers, and to the volunteers ministering to them.

Before considering educational outreaches, support groups, and respite ministry, talk to the caregivers in your church to find out what is most needed and investigate what other options are already available in your immediate area. There may be an abundance of caregiver outreach programs in your area and what is needed most by your members is a directory of services.

Three Other Ways to Support Caregivers.

1. Meals and grocery shopping. "Caregivers lose their independence, and while it's important for them to get out and have some downtime, regular trips to the grocery store can be a challenge."
2. Send a financial service. "Many caregivers find themselves in the uncomfortable role of managing someone else's finances.

Budgets, long-term planning, filing taxes, medical bills and other financial matters can pile up on a caregiver quickly."

3. Home maintenance. "Just like the caregiver's physical health, the state of the house can also show wear and tear. Cleaning gutters, lawn care, weeding, minor repairs, even building a wheelchair ramp are helpful ways a local church can effectively serve their members, and even non-members who are in the community."

Peter Rosenberger, 2009. "5 Ways the Church Can Help Caregivers". Indiana Bible College Apostolic Information Service

14

Community of Watchmen

IN CHAPTER 6, THE challenges of elder abuse, fraud and exploitation and their devastating consequences were identified. So what role can communities of faith play in protecting older adults? There are four ways to disrupt cycles of abuse and exploitation:

1. Awareness and recognizing signs
2. Policies and procedures on reporting
3. Congregational education and creating a culture of protection
4. Interventional programs

Chapter 6 identified the various types of abuse, neglect, fraud, and exploitation, but it is necessary to also understand the many warning signs and red flags which may signal that elder abuse is occurring. According to the U.S. Department of Justice's Elder Justice Initiative[1], here are the warning signs to be aware of:

Physical Abuse:

1. Bruises, black eyes, welts, lacerations, or rope marks
2. Bone fractures, broken bones, or skull fractures

---

1. See U.S. Dept of Justice, "Red Flags of Elde Abuse"

3. Open wounds, cuts, punctures, untreated injuries in various stages of healing
4. Sprains, dislocations, or internal injuries/bleeding
5. Broken eyeglasses/frames, physical signs of being subjected to punishment, or signs of being restrained
6. Laboratory findings of medication overdose or under-utilization of prescribed drugs
7. An older adult's sudden change in behavior
8. The caregiver's refusal to allow visitors to see or speak to an older adult alone
9. An older adult's report of being hit, slapped, kicked, or mistreated

Emotional Abuse:

1. Being emotionally upset or agitated
2. Being extremely withdrawn, non-communicative, or non-responsive
3. Unusual behavior, such as sucking, biting, rocking
4. Witnessing a caregiver controlling or isolating an older adult
5. Exhibiting a change in sleeping patterns or eating habits
6. Personality changes, such as apologizing excessively
7. Depression or anxiety
8. An older adult's report of being verbally or emotionally mistreated

Financial Exploitation:

1. Sudden changes in bank accounts or banking practices, including an unexplained withdrawal of large sums of money by a person accompanying the older adult
2. The inclusion of additional names on an older adult's bank signature card
3. Unauthorized withdrawal of the older adult's funds using their ATM card
4. Abrupt changes in a will or other financial documents
5. Unexplained disappearance of funds or valuable possessions

6. Provision of substandard care or bills left unpaid despite the availability of adequate financial resources
7. Discovery of a forged signature for financial transactions or for the titles of the older adult's possessions
8. Sudden appearance of previously uninvolved relatives claiming their rights to an older adult's property or possessions
9. Unexplained sudden transfer of assets to a family member or someone outside the family
10. The provision of services that are not necessary
11. An older adult's report of financial exploitation
12. Unexplained credit card charges

Neglect & Abandonment:

1. Dehydration, malnutrition, untreated bed sores, and poor personal hygiene
2. Unattended or untreated health problems
3. Hazardous or unsafe living conditions/arrangements (e.g., improper wiring, no heat, or no running water)
4. Unsanitary and unclean living conditions (e.g., dirt, fleas, lice on person, soiled bedding, fecal/urine smell, inadequate clothing)
5. The desertion of an older adult at a hospital, a nursing facility, or other similar institution, or a shopping center or other public location
6. An older adult's report of being neglected or abandoned
7. Lack of food in the refrigerator or cupboards

Sexual Abuse:

1. Bruises around the breasts or genital area
2. Unexplained venereal disease or genital infections
3. Unexplained vaginal or anal bleeding
4. Changes in an older adult's demeanor, such as showing fear or becoming withdrawn when a specific person is around
5. Evidence of pornographic material being shown to an older adult with diminished capacity

6. Blood found on sheets, linens or an older adult's clothing
7. An older adult's report of being sexually assaulted or raped

SafeSeniorCare.com[2] also points out that sometimes "symptoms of abuse may manifest as vague behavior changes, which might be hard to distinguish from symptoms of dementia or depression. Pay attention to any intuitive feelings that something may be wrong in a senior's situation. Some of the more general signs that something is wrong could include:

1. Sudden changes in behavior, such as becoming more nervous, jumpy, aggressive or withdrawn
2. Losing interest in favorite activities
3. Difficulty sleeping
4. Unexplained or sudden weight loss
5. Any of these changes could indicate that an elder is emotionally distraught, which could be a result of physical, emotional or sexual abuse.

It also could mean that some of their needs are being neglected. For example, weight loss could indicate that their nutritional needs are changing and that the change is being overlooked. Other signs that should raise some red flags to possible abuse could include:

1. Increased nervousness around a particular caregiver
2. Hostility or frustration in the relationships between an elder and the caregiver
3. Threatening, controlling or demeaning behavior from the caregiver towards the elder
4. A caregiver who won't permit the elder to be alone with trusted friends and family members

> 4 Ways to Prevent Elder Abuse.
>
> 5. Stay Connected. Keep in touch with families, friends, and neighbors as much as possible. Stay in touch with the church. One of the hallmarks of abuse is isolation, and being in contact

2. See Laura Herman, "7 Forms of Elder Abuse"

with a number of different people and entities can help reduce the likelihood that a person could be abused.

6. Stay Organized. Keep belongings neat; keep track of possessions; open and send your own mail; direct deposit Social Security and other checks; complete and sign your own checks whenever possible; use an answering machine to screen calls and if possible, do not provide personal information over the telephone or computer.

7. Stay Informed. Consult with an attorney about future plans, including executing a power of attorney; consult with an attorney about caregiving arrangements; review your will; know where to go if you suspect abuse; ask for help from the church, from police, from Adult Protective Services, or if necessary, employees at a bank.

8. Stay Alert. Do not leave items of value out in the open; do not sign any document unless someone you trust reviews it; do not be left out of decisions about your finances or other important parts of your life. Families, particularly those who find themselves in a caregiving role, also need to be aware of situations that place their older loved ones at risk for abuse.

Dr. Ken Ford, "Elder Abuse". EpiscopalChurch.org

An article in *Ministry Magazine* indicated that clergy "are one of the most likely groups of professionals to encounter cases of elder abuse" and that "reporting elder abuse is the act of a responsible person trying to assist an older person in crisis"[3] If your place of worship does not already have policies and procedures in place to report suspected instances of abuse or neglect (which can be done anonymously), it is worth it to talk to your leadership about implementing such policies. Every state has a toll-free number or hotline to report suspected abuse cases, so adding that number for your particular area would be a logical addition to your policies. If a person is living in assisted living, memory care, or a nursing home, a report of potential abuse or neglect can also be made to your local Long-Term Care Ombudsman. Facilities are required to post the ombudsman contact information in a well-placed area, but the local information can also be found at the National Long-Term Care Ombudsman Resource Center (NORC.ACL.gov).

3. See Weaver and Koenig, "Elder Abuse"

Scams and fraud have different reporting methods. If an older adult thinks they have been a victim of a scam, it should be reported to both your local police department and the Federal Trade Commission. It would be helpful for your policies and procedures to include not only the contact information for those two reporting authorities, but also a list of basic questions to ask someone who has been victimized to help make the reporting easier and less intimidating. Questions such as, "What was the phone number this person called from?", "What did they sound like on the phone (i.e. did they speak with an accent)?", "What did they say to you?", "What did they make you believe would happen?", "Do you still have the email they sent?" can all go a long way towards possibly catching the perpetrators. Offering to help the older adult make the report would also be best practice.

There are several training programs that can be utilized to help congregations learn more about elder abuse and exploitation.

1. The National Center on Elder Abuse offers plain language articles and handouts, as well as resources on reporting, and recognizing World Elder Abuse Awareness Day. Their website is NCEA.ACL.gov
2. The Federal Trade Commission has Consumer Alert newsletters, the Do Not Call Registry, and free credit report access, as well as the national fraud complaint center. They also have free publications about various scams and fraud that can be ordered in bulk. Their website is FTC.gov
3. The Better Business Bureau in your area can provide a speaker for an educational seminar on the latest scams and fraud. Their website is BBB.org

Faith communities can also foster safe spaces for victims to tell their story because a pastor or church member may be the only social contact an older adult has with the outside world. The article in Ministry Magazine also stated that "an additional element in preventing elder abuse is the significant religious value which teaches that no one should be subjected to abusive or neglectful behavior. It is natural for faith communities to hold and promote these values. When older adults are regarded as disposable, society fails to recognize the importance of assuring dignified and respectful living situations for all. In addition to promoting positive social attitudes toward seniors, faith communities can take positive steps to educate people about elder maltreatment and to encourage interventions, which help families cope with problems that contribute to abuse."

Part 2: Finding Solutions

A couple of interventional programs that could be established in your congregation are the Friendly Visitor program in which church members regularly visit homebound and older congregation members (not necessarily for a respite, just a check-in), and a Parish/Denomination Nurse Ministry, "in which a knowledgeable and professional health care worker can help educate the congregation as well as be an observer of the needs of homebound members"[4] If there is suspected abuse or neglect going on in the home, a friendly visit from church members or bringing of sacraments may be the one opportunity an astute observation can be made and reported to authorities.

Rev. Dr. Richard Gentzler also summed up a faith institution's role in disrupting elder abuse. He stated, "Church leaders can help prevent abuse by teaching older adults and their families how to report fraud (especially telemarketing fraud), informing them about the types and signs of elder abuse; and encouraging those with family members in nursing homes to visit them often; if a family member is a caregiver, encourage and support the caregiver in getting respite."

By becoming aware of the signs of abuse, neglect, and exploitation, establishing reporting procedures, providing community education, and checking in on homebound older adults, faith communities can foster a community of watchmen that look out for the best interests of their congregation's most vulnerable adults.

Sources for Training.

1. Department of Justice SAFE (Safe Accessible Forensic Interviewing for Elders) Training. The one-day course begins with a brief introduction to the concept of elder abuse (history, statistics), then transitions to exploring the ways in which elder abuse dynamics and aspects of aging impact communicating with older adults. The training includes interactive activities. Contact elder.justice@usdoj.gov
2. The Better Business Bureau can provide community training on recognizing and responding to scams and fraud.

---

4. See The United Methodist Church Discipleship Ministries, "Elder Abuse: The Role of Church Leaders"

15

Healing the Family

WHILE MOST CLERGY HAVE probably had some basic training in pastoral counseling, that training may not have covered some of the complex issues that arise between aging parents and their adult children. And while deep-seated, unresolved feelings are probably best left to mental health professionals, members of clergy can help families at least get on the same page and open up a deeper level of understanding of each other's concerns.

> A 2023 study of parent and adult child estrangement published in the Journal of Marriage and Family reported 6% of people estranged from their mother and 26% estranged from their father. However, of those with a history of estrangement, 81% reconciled with their mother and 69% reconciled with their father. *American Psychological Association*

One unique tool that clergy can employ in pastoral counseling that can help adult children and caregivers better manage their expectations of what their loved one can do is called Spoon Theory. The term "Spoon Theory" was coined by writer Christine Miserandino while trying to explain to a friend what her life was like while trying to live with a chronic disability. The theory states that each person wakes up every day with a certain number of spoons, wherein the spoon is just a measure of units of energy. A person who is able-bodied may wake up with, say, 24 spoons (or 24 units of energy). As they go about their day, they use their spoons for various tasks. For example, taking a shower make take 1 spoon; making coffee may take 1 spoon; checking work emails may take 2 spoons; cooking dinner may take 3 spoons; etc. At the end of the day, they may have some spoons, or reserve energy, left over.

However, a person with a disability, chronic pain, or dementia may only wake up with 12 spoons (or 12 units of energy). For them, each task requires more effort than the able-bodied person. For example, taking a shower may require 4 spoons; eating breakfast may take 2 spoons; putting on clothes may take 3 spoons, etc. They run out of energy before the day is even halfway over. Spoon theory helps a caregiver or adult child better empathize with their loved one about what tasks can be reasonably accomplished, what tasks may require extra help or extra time, and why some people get more irritable or agitated in the late afternoon/early evening hours ("sundowning"). The theory can also help caregivers understand why their loved one may be unmotivated to do certain things, which a caregiver might misinterpret as "lazy", and help adjust schedules and routines to times of day when their loved one has more energy.

Another good use of Spoon Theory is for caregivers who are juggling the demands of caring for their loved one, work, and obligations to their own families. Understanding that they only have so many spoons to utilize during the day may help prevent caregiver burnout; "Learning to say "no" to some things, to say "yes" to others is an important lifelong skill. While the world doesn't stop spinning for any of us based on our unique personal needs, pain, and limitations require a sense of self-compassion. Spoon theory can be a tool in our lifestyle toolbox to help others understand the need to exercise self-care and self-compassion"[1]

Another unique tool that families can use to change the way they communicate is called the Aikido of Communication. This communication technique for de-escalating conflict was developed by Judy Ringer, a second-degree black belt in Aikido. According to Ringer, "Aikido also physically embodies critical communication skills, such as active listening, empathy and perspective taking, and offers ways to re-pattern unhelpful communication habits. For example, in everyday life, the Aikido metaphor plays out when you acknowledge someone's comments and paraphrase what you hear. You're also practicing communication Aikido whenever you listen with curiosity to an opposing view or search for mutual

---

1. See Chris Prange-Morgan, "What Is "Spoon Theory"?

understanding, respect and purpose"[2] There are four main principles to the Aikido of Communication:

1. Reframing- instead of resisting what another person is saying, try to connect with what they are saying by reframing what you heard. For example, one might say, "You sound concerned that the direction we're taking may not be the best one".

2. Non-Judgement- making snap judgements and forgone conclusions about another person leaves us with an inability to see any other perspective. "Once we judge someone as a problem, that's all we see in them, and we miss their more open, empathetic parts".

3. Curiosity and Inquiry- being sincere and asking honest, open-ended questions can lead to a much deeper level of understanding. Questions such as, "What do you think is the best solution here?" or "What would you like me to do differently?" invites people to really share what is on their hearts and minds.

4. Appreciation- it may sound counterintuitive to appreciate conflict, but in this instance, appreciation means helping another person to identify his or her resistance and turn it into an opportunity for dissolving conflict. Our skill in communication lies in our ability to identify the resistance and help the communicator to express it. "For example, "I'm not sure I understand, can you say more?" Without something to push against, the resistance turns into energy we can join and lead toward further understanding and problem solving."

Ringer goes on to add that once there is an opening to share your viewpoint, there are four more steps that can help communicate why you feel the way you do:

1. Educate- don't assume that another person has the same frame of reference as you. Teach them what things look like from your perspective.

2. Communicate your hopes and goals- explain to the other person what it is you hope to accomplish, or your goals for a particular outcome.

3. Remain Curious- stay open-minded to different possibilities and different perspectives.

4. Center Yourself and Extend Positive Energy- stay focused on a mutually beneficial outcome, honor others' viewpoints, and stay flexible.

2. See Judy Ringer, "The Aikido of Communication"

Part 2: Finding Solutions

For families, this style of conflict resolution may help break down barriers to care. If a mom can no longer safely stay at home and needs to move to assisted living but is refusing to move, the adult child can employ these techniques to understand the mom's fears and feelings about moving. Conversely, the child can communicate to mom more effectively the concerns for her safety and their hopes that she can thrive in a new environment, rather than just survive in her current environment.

> Misconceptions and myths about what is normal for the aging process, options for care and how to pay for them, estate plans, and dementia can all play a pivotal role in family stress. Can your faith community host a series of lectures on topics related to aging? Invite local professionals to speak to your congregation on topics such as Wills, Trusts, & Estate Plans, Assisted Living vs. Nursing Homes, The Aging Process, Dementia vs. Normal Aging, Medicare & Medicaid, and other timely topics. Often a neutral third party with professional experience can be the thing that gets families moving in the same direction.

A third unique tool that is especially good for helping families establish and maintain boundaries is assertiveness training. Assertiveness training can help families identify in themselves whether they are passive or aggressive, in which circumstances and around which people, and then build a bridge between the two extremes. People who are passive tend to "give in to other people's wishes while forgetting their own needs and wants; have a difficult time saying no to people; often have a hard time making decisions; have a hard time maintaining eye contact; avoid confrontation at all costs"[3] Conversely, those who are aggressive tend to "be concerned only for their needs at the expense of others' needs; have a tendency to lose their temper; may make decisions for other people; may shout or use bully techniques to get their way; may continue to argue long after someone has had enough; may call others names or even use obscenities when angry; may openly criticize or find fault with others ideas, opinions, or behaviors; often use confrontation to get what they want" Sometimes a person can be both passive and aggressive about some circumstances or with certain people without even knowing it. Familial relationships are complicated due to their intimate, lifelong, and evolving nature, so passivity and aggressiveness can ebb and flow over time. However, the happy medium is found in assertiveness. People who are assertive "are concerned with both their

---

3. See AtHealth.com, "Assertiveness"

needs as well as other people's needs; are openly able to express themselves with other people; are able to respond in a respectful manner when there is a disagreement; are able to ask for help; are confident and able to make decisions; are able to say no to people/places/things they do not want; are responsible for their own feelings/behaviors/thoughts". In their book, *Asserting Yourself-Updated Edition: A Practical Guide For Positive Change*, Sharon and Gordon Bower help people understand how to communicate more assertively with the DESC script:

D- Describe the situation objectively and factually

E- Express your feelings about the situation using "I" statements

S- Specify what outcome you desire

C- Specify both the positive and negative consequences

For example, if siblings are in conflict over the responsibility of dad's care, a DESC script may look something like "I've had to take dad to his last 3 doctor appointments by myself. As a result, I had to use three of my sick days from work. I would like the two of us to take turns getting dad to his appointments. Otherwise, I will run out of sick days and all the responsibility will fall on you."

> Managing Expectations for Someone With Cognitive Impairment. A person who has a loss of cognition can often no longer communicate the way he or she always has. It is not unusual for them to exhibit bad judgement, inability to follow multi-step directions, paranoia/accusations, and inability to follow logic. The loss of these abilities is often mystifying, confusing, and frustrating for both the person experiencing impairment and the person trying to communicate with them. However, understanding the loss of key abilities related to thinking can help the person trying to communicate be more empathetic and take a different approach. For example, if a loved one accuses you of stealing their wallet when in fact they were the one who misplaced it, offer to help him look for it. Arguing with someone who has no ability to use logic only makes matters worse. A better approach is to make your request look like something that would be fun or would be doing you a favor. For example, if your loved one refuses to take a shower, make the experience feel like a spa day for a special occasion, complete with warm fluffy robe, hand and foot massage, etc. Another approach to use is shifting responsibility to a trusted authority figure. Instead of arguing with your loved one about taking their

Part 2: Finding Solutions

medications, remind them that their doctor, for whom they have respect, told them the medications were necessary.

A useful tool to address grief is Grief Share classes. These classes can be held in-person or virtually and cover a variety of topics over 13 weeks. The Grief Share program is specific to the loss of a loved one, but it may make it possible for the door to be opened on different causes of grief. Perhaps your faith community can host the classes or connect members to another local group.

It is also worth noting that facilitating end-of-life decision making may help resolve family conflicts as well, especially ones related to estate planning. Having an elder law attorney come and speak to your faith community about important documents such as advanced directives, powers of attorney, wills, trusts, and conservatorships/guardianships can lead families to greater understanding of all their options and put to bed common misconceptions that produce feelings of frustration and mistrust. Inviting a hospice social worker to speak about hospice and palliative care can help families make informed choices about their options for end-of-life care. Other tools for facilitating end-of-life decisions include The Five Wishes, which guides families through the advanced directive in plain language and is legal in all 50 states, and PrepareForYourCare.org, which provides guidance through videos and is available in languages other than English. Both of these tools are listed in the Resources section of this book.

These tools, along with pastoral counseling techniques can help families improve lines of communication, empathize with each other, and get a better understanding of their own thoughts, feelings, and motivations.

> Facilitating the Conversation About Death. Most people are uncomfortable talking about death, but it may help to have a congregational workshop to open the lines of communication and help people feel more prepared. Try incorporating:
>
> 1. Explanation of types of funeral services in your tradition
> 2. Choices for suggested Scripture readings
> 3. Variety of suggested hymns and musical selections
> 4. Remarks of remembrances (who, how many, how long)
> 5. Who to call, and when, after a death occurs
> 6. Fees, if any, associated with using your church building
> 7. Repast or reception: does your church offer volunteers to help?
> 8. Appropriate honorariums for minister, musicians or others

9. Information on your state's advance directive requirements
10. Advance directive workbooks, such as Five Wishes
11. Local hospice organization brochures
12. Local home health organization brochures
13. Listing of cemeteries and funeral homes

Lauren Hales, "Congregational Conversations on Death and Dying". Church Health Center, ChurchHealth.org

16

Other Solutions

THREE CHALLENGES WERE OUTLINED in Chapter 8 regarding food insecurity, housing insecurity, and transportation. Communities of faith, by their very nature of creating places of belonging and connection, are exceptionally positioned to assist in mitigating these three challenges.

> The 2018 National Congregations Study indicated that "48% of U.S. congregations either had their own food-distribution program or supported efforts run by another organization, such as a food bank or food pantry. That's over 150,000 congregations."
> TheConversation.com, October 28, 2021

When it comes to food insecurity, there are a few options that your faith community might consider, including a food pantry, a food redistribution ministry, a meal delivery service, and a Little Free Pantry. Many places of worship have food pantries that are open to the community. If your faith community is considering a food pantry, here are some practical steps to follow:

1. Conduct a needs assessment of your members to find out exactly what help is needed most. Also take stock of the existing food pantries in your area; rather than start your own, could you support them in their effort?

Other Solutions

2. Talk to your members and get their support. According to an article on SuperFoodHelp.com, "Garnering support for the food pantry project involves transparent communication, highlighting the importance of addressing food insecurity and showcasing how everyone's contribution can make a significant difference. Encouraging active participation from church members through volunteering, donations, or spreading awareness can create a strong foundation for the success of your food pantry initiative."[1]

3. Set up your space and the logistics of your pantry. Keep in mind the need for space, parking, foot traffic flow, volunteer schedules, and the efficiency of the pickup process. Some good points to consider include whether your pantry intends to distribute pre-packed bags or boxes or allow patrons to come in and select their own items.

4. Form partnerships with food banks and other organizations that can supply food for distribution. Could your church or synagogue partner with a school, university, or businesses for regular food drives?

5. Establish guidelines for eligibility. Will there be an application process? What are the criteria for income and household size? How do you determine who is most in need? SuperFoodHelp.com recommends "establish[ing] transparent and consistent procedures for verifying eligibility, which can help prevent misuse of resources and ensure that support reaches those who truly need it. Additionally, creating fair distribution practices, such as implementing a first-come, first-served system or prioritizing vulnerable populations, can help promote equity and accessibility in the distribution of food items". It would also be worthwhile to establish guidelines surrounding the delivery of food items to those who are homebound.

6. Promote your food pantry in the community through marketing efforts on social media, flyers, and outreach events.

7. Also consider if your faith institution plans to use the food pantry as an opportunity to minister to others through offering prayers, personal invitations to services, distributions of sacred texts, etc.

If opening a food pantry to the community is not feasible for your place of worship, or you don't want to duplicate efforts already in place in your area, perhaps think about having a bookcase or small closet of

---

1. "How to Start a Food Pantry at Your Church", See SuperFoodHelp.com

shelf-stable food items for use by members who need a little extra help from time to time.

> Quick Facts on Food Waste.
> 1. "It is currently estimated that more than 10 billion pounds of food are left in the field and never harvested, usually referred to as a "walk-by" field by farmers." 1
> 2. "In 2018, it was estimated that tomato farmers in Florida left 4% of crops in the field, lettuce farmers in Arizona left 56% of crops in the field, and peach farmers in New Jersey left 40% of crops in the field." 1
> 3. "EPA estimates that in 2019, 66.2 million tons of wasted food was generated in the food retail, food service, and residential sectors. Of this, 40% was from households, 40% was from food service providers, and 20% was from food retail. Most of this waste (59.8%) was landfilled." 2
>
> 1. 2020 Gleaning Census. NationalGleaningProject.org
> 2. 2019 Wasted Food Report. EPA.gov

Another type of food distribution is a redistribution, or gleaning ministry. Gleaning involves partnering with farms, farmers markets, and grocery stores to redistribute unsold produce to those in need. The Center for Agriculture and Food Systems has a resource database that includes gleaning-related laws, a map of existing gleaning organizations, and research-based reports. The food gleaned can be distributed in the same way as an organized food pantry, or your faith community may partner with local senior living facilities that provide subsidized housing for older adults. Keep in mind that food gleaning most often involves fresh produce, prepared foods, and other items that may spoil without refrigeration, and the amount of any one item gleaned may not be enough to distribute evenly to everyone who comes to the distribution, so it is important to have policies in place that make things as equitable as possible. The space or vehicle from which you distribute goods must also have refrigeration capabilities, or coolers large enough to store items.

A meal delivery ministry could be a great way to minister to those who are homebound and fill in the gaps left by public Meals on Wheels programs which may not be available in all areas or even have a waitlist.

Other Solutions

The meal delivery ministry could meet weekly and prepare meals in large batches that are packaged and delivered to homebound members, who can then simply microwave a meal at home. They can even recycle the food packaging so that when a congregation member comes to deliver the next week's meals, they can also pick up the previous week's containers. One subsidized senior apartment building had within its own tenants a "peanut butter and jelly committee" who met weekly on Fridays to make sandwiches for other older tenants who were homebound and would not receive Meals on Wheels on the weekends.

An important point for consideration is older adults' attitudes towards accepting help and charity. Recent research indicates that nearly half of older adults are not using the government benefits available to them, and one of the reasons is because they feel that by accepting help for themselves, it takes benefits away from others[2] One possible solution to circumvent a resistance to help is by installing a Little Free Pantry or Blessing Box at your place of worship. The premise of the Little Free Pantry is the same as the Little Free Library program; people can take what they need and leave some for others. Little Free Pantries enable older adults to leave some items they might not be able to eat (such as certain items in commodity food boxes) and exchange them for things they can eat. Being able to contribute instead of just receiving can protect an older adult's dignity while still giving them access to the food they need. Another benefit is that people can utilize the box at any time, rather than wait for a certain time and day for the food pantry distribution. Little Free Pantries can be made from lumber, recycled cabinetry, recycled newspaper dispensing machines, old refrigerators, etc. and can make a wonderful project for an Eagle Scout in your congregation.

---

2. See National Council on Aging, "Seniors & SNAP"

Part 2: Finding Solutions

This Little Free Pantry was made from a recycled newspaper dispenser

The challenge of housing insecurity for older adults may require some more out-of-the-box, grassroots thinking. Most faith communities probably do not have the financial means to build housing for older adults in need, but some are leasing out unused land and partnering with nonprofits to build affordable housing on ground that is sitting idle. Some cities are converting church buildings into affordable apartments rather than letting them go to waste.

Another trend is co-housing, in which a group of like-minded individuals build homes surrounding a central hub so that they can create their own supportive micro-community to enable aging in place. Models of co-housing can range from a circle of tiny homes around a hub where people can gather for meals, laundry, and activities, to full sized homes on quarter

Other Solutions

acre lots. The advantages of co-housing include reduced social isolation, leveraging the abilities of group members to assist each other, and even strengthening spiritual ties. The Co-Housing Association of the U.S. has a directory of existing co-housing villages and resources for those interested in building their own.

Another grassroots trend is aging-in-place village networks in which older adults pay an annual membership fee to their network, and in exchange receive services such as care navigation, home modifications, referrals to vetted service providers, phone and home visit check-ins, social activities, transportation and more. These networks aim to provide assistance for older adults so they can remain in their own homes longer rather than having to move to a senior living facility. This model works well for smaller geographical footprints, such as a rural area, a suburb, or neighborhood within a city.

> Trends in Church-to-Housing Conversions. "In Seattle, and in many places, planners and congregations are eyeing empty church parking lots for redevelopment. "Faith institutions that have these large parking lots are driven by a vision of maintaining their properties, staying in the neighborhood, and continuing to serve affordable housing or other services," says Stephanie Velasco, housing levy communications manager with the Office of Housing in Seattle.
>
> The city has identified about 300 acres of church-owned land (out of a total 53,163 acres) and is offering a density bonus to churches that develop affordable housing on their land. Importantly, there's a movement to redevelop Black-owned church properties to create affordable housing in Seattle; Oakland, California; and Washington, D.C." American Planning Association, "Transforming Empty Churches Into Affordable Housing Takes More Than a Leap of Faith". Planning.org

However, there are a couple of solutions that any faith community can easily put into place. One solution is a housing directory that lists different available housing and approximate price points. A directory might include HUD subsidized apartments, market-rate apartment complexes, assisted living and memory care facilities, as well as 55+ communities. Be sure to include any pertinent information regarding address, contact information, application procedures, pet policies, etc. The directory could perhaps even include a list of resources for those who desire to stay at home that includes non-medical home care agencies, transportation providers, meal

Part 2: Finding Solutions

delivery services, etc. A second solution is a house-sharing matchup. Many older adults find that letting out rooms in their house to other older adults not only reduces expenses but prevents social isolation (think *The Golden Girls*). Perhaps space could be made available on a bulletin board for those seeking roommates, or who have a mother-in-law suite to rent. Nesterly.com is a house-sharing matchup service that is available in some areas and growing nationwide that can pair those with extra room with seekers of affordable housing. A third solution might be a handyperson ministry that can help older adults age-in-place in their own homes by providing small home repairs, building a wheelchair ramp, etc., or partnering with Habitat for Humanity's Aging in Place program.

Transportation challenges also have some solutions. Many faith communities already have a bus ministry to provide transportation for members in need of a ride. If your place of worship is considering purchasing a bus, be mindful of the long-term costs for maintenance and insurance, as well as policies for driving and maintaining it. If that is not an option for your faith community, perhaps a carpooling option would work better. Those in need of a ride to church can be matched up with those in their zip code or neighborhood who are willing to offer rides. It can even be as simple as posting side-by-side lists on a bulletin board, with one list for ride seekers and one list for ride givers. Ride share options such as Uber and Lyft are widely available, but there is one ride share program designed specifically for older adults called Go Go Grandparent. It uses many of the same drivers as Uber and Lyft, but rather than having to navigate an app, riders can call a 1–800 number to schedule transportation. It is subscription-based, so caregivers can pre-load dollar amounts onto their loved one's account for local trips. The website is listed in the Resources section of this book.

> Shared Mobility. In areas with low walkability and limited public transportation, could the faith community be the missing link in mobility? "Church-based transportation aims to convert church parking lots into transportation hubs in underserved communities. Given that church parking lots are often unused gray space during weekdays, the opportunity for repurposing that space for the service of nearby neighborhoods could transform shared mobility access." Houses of worship located near bus and train stops could serve as park-and-ride stations or provide shuttle service to those stops. Curtis M. Tyger, 2019. "Church-Based Transportation: A New Shared Mobility Service That Converts Church Parking Lots into Transportation Hubs for Metro Atlanta

Communities", Georgia Institute of Technology School of City and Regional Planning

These suggestions draw upon connecting members together to mitigate problems, which increases the feeling of community and belonging. Building connections to each other and being in community with other believers is literally one of the cornerstones that faith communities are built on, but the current state of aging is forcing houses of worship to reimagine what those connections could look like.

Part 2 Conclusion

PART 2 OF THIS book looked at a variety of responses to each of the eleven challenges outlined in Part 1 - falls, dementia, vision and hearing loss, social isolation, caregiving, abuse and exploitation, relationship problems, food insecurity, housing insecurity, and transportation.

Part 1 concluded that each of those challenges had direct effects on the others, further complicating each already complicated issue. The result looked like a chaotic mess:

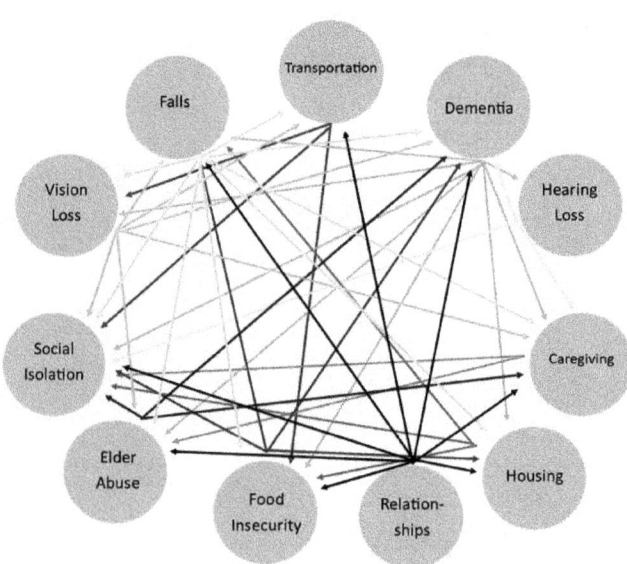

Part 2 Conclusion

Part 2 identified ways faith communities can play a role in mitigating these challenges in different ways that are applicable to their congregation's specific needs and capabilities. Places of worship are the perfect places to implement these cycle-disrupting solutions and help older adults flourish in this stage of life. Now rather than looking like a chaotic mess, faith communities can bring order and peace to the aging process:

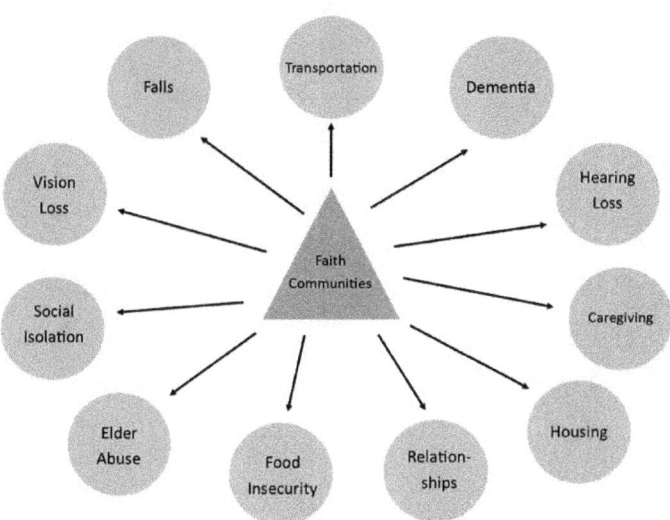

The visual that this chart represents is reminiscent of a quote by Corrie Ten Boom: "If you look at the world, you'll be distressed. If you look within, you'll be depressed. If you look at God, you'll be at rest". What started out as looking like the bleak years, now looks more like the golden years that older people have lived and worked for their entire lives. For so long, communities of faith have been silos focused on spiritual nourishment once or twice a week and evangelism with some mission work sprinkled in, looking in from the outside at the social challenges of older adults. Now faith communities have the opportunity to do what they were designed to do in the beginning, which is be the center of the body of believers, moving members towards each other and towards God.

PART 3

Challenge as Opportunity

"Is not wisdom found among the aged? Does not long life bring understanding?"
—Job 12:12 (NIV)

17

Intergenerational Connections

ONE HURDLE THAT NEARLY every faith community experiences is how to connect older and younger members together. Older members may obviously serve in leadership roles in children and youth ministry but rarely do any other intergenerational lines cross. The result is that children/youth ministries and older adult ministries operate in silos, reflective of trends that are seen in the larger society of families who are spread out all across the country and a disconnect between grandparents and grandchildren. This disconnection leads to younger generations having no idea of how to treat older adults, nor of how to learn from them.

However, despite this challenge there is an opportunity for faith communities to disrupt the cycle and create a more family-like atmosphere where both older and younger generations can learn from each other. The effect is that younger generations can have the benefit of not only learning from older adults but also having a support system of stand-in grandparents to mentor them through life's challenges. The benefit for older adults is being able to learn new things from them as well as having a new network of support to aid in some of the tasks they can no longer do alone. The benefits for both groups are a new level of understanding, a new sense of purpose, and stronger social connections. A report by LifelongFaith.com also identified key benefits to intergenerational ministry: "it strengthens faith and involvement for all ages, provides relationships beyond family, utilizes gifts and abilities of all, forms caring community, and passes on

Part 3: Challenge as Opportunity

faith traditions."[1] Rev. Corbin Kill of First United Pentecostal Church of Quitman, Mississippi remarked on the benefits of an intergenerational community of faith in a survey for this book by stating that "Our elders are precious witnesses that give living testimony that speaks to the younger generations- we did it, we have made it this far, so can you".

> "Many researchers have recognized that interactions between people of different generations are key to reducing age discrimination and the social isolation of older people."
> *International Journal of Environmental Research and Public Health*

The book *Lifelong Faith Formation for All Ages and Generations* by John Roberto[2] outlines a roadmap that churches and synagogues can use to create or enhance an intergenerational culture. Here are the 9 steps faith communities can follow:

1. Form an intergenerational task force representing the essential ministries of the church and be sure that all the generations are included from youth to older adults.

2. Develop a vision—with short descriptive sentences—of what an intergenerational church culture can look like in three years.

3. Explore the opportunities for building an intergenerational approach throughout church life.

    - Identify ministries, programs, and activities that are already intergenerational (with generations building relationships, learning, praying, worshipping, serving, and/or leading together); and develop strategies for strengthening and expanding intergenerational ministries, programs, and activities.

    - Identify ministries, programs, and activities that are multigenerational (with all ages present without the intergenerational connection and experiences) that can be transformed into more intentionally intergenerational experiences.

    - Identify age-specific ministries, programs, and activities that can be redesigned by including additional generations, building intergenerational relationships, engaging in intergenerational experiences, and more

---

1. See Kehrwald and Roberto, "Insights from Research & Theory: Practices for Forming Faith Intergenerationally"

2. See John Roberto, *Lifelong Faith Formation for All Ages and Generations*

- Identify new opportunities for creating intergenerational experiences by intentionally designing programs, activities, and ministries to meet this objective.

4. Generate a variety of ideas and projects that the church can develop in each of the four categories: strengthening intergenerational opportunities, transforming multigenerational opportunities, redesigning age-specific opportunities, and designing new initiatives.

5. Create a three-year plan by selecting projects that fulfill the vision and provide practical ways to develop an intergenerational culture. A three-year plan allows you to identify projects that can be implemented in the short term (first year), and projects that need more time for design and implementation over the three years.

6. Present the plan to church leaders and the community. Make a solid case for the need to be intergenerational and the blessings and benefits that it will bring to the church community. Share the plan: your goals and short-term and long-term projects. Invite feedback, suggestions, and ideas.

7. Implement your plan. Short-term projects can be launched quickly. Long-term projects may need to be piloted with a small group of your target audience (a version 1.0 of the project) to test its effectiveness and then modify it for launch on a wider scale.

8. Continue to evaluate your efforts but be patient. Each effort provides new learning that can be used to continue to move toward becoming a more intentionally intergenerational church.

9. Keep innovating! Introduce new projects and programs each year. Communicate the stories and examples of the benefits and blessings that are coming to the church community because of the intergenerational focus.

> What Science Says About Intergenerational Culture. "Establishing the mentor/teacher learning model allows older adults to be reminded and to appreciate the life experiences they faced and the skills they learned from it in order to help serve as a guide to the coming generations. Likewise, older adults gain the opportunity to share their skills and learn about the contemporary youth and their behaviors and personalities. Results of these programs have shown improvements in younger individuals' self-esteem, interest levels

Part 3: Challenge as Opportunity

in subjects such as language arts, attendance rates in schools, and in their literacy levels. Older adults also reported a 56% positive change in attitudes towards children and a 73% increase in overall satisfaction with life and wellbeing." Satya Moolani, 2020. "The Value of Intergenerational Relationships" ChangingAging.org

The Christian Reformed Church has a comprehensive Intergenerational Church Toolkit that includes tons of information and resources on the how's and why's of intergenerational ministry, books, articles, websites, questions to consider, examples from other faith communities, videos, webinars, ideas, curriculums, and much more. Their website is CRCNA.org and is listed in the Resources section of this book.

There are many practical ideas that places of worship can use for intentional intergenerational ministry. Beaver Baptist Church in Brighton, Tennessee has a program called "Titus 2 Tuesdays when older ladies share a craft or skill with younger ladies like a holiday recipe, canning produce, or sewing garments." One way that faith communities can strengthen intergenerational bonds is through a class called "Now & Then". The Now & Then class is a purposeful intergenerational class that could meet during weekend or weekday education times for a period of 6 weeks. The premise of the class is how older and younger members can learn new things from each other as well as find their common ground in faith. Here are some suggestions for how the class might operate:

1. Older members teach younger members how to tie a necktie and present themselves for a job interview; younger members teach older members tips on using their email; both groups compare what it's like to have a job and things they learned on the job; both groups discuss what sacred texts say about how work glorifies God.

2. Older members teach younger members how to cook a meal; younger members teach older members tips on using their cell phones; both groups compare favorite recipes, memories of special meals, things they've learned through cooking, etc.; both group discuss what sacred texts say about the importance of fellowship with other believers.

3. Older members teach younger members what it means to have good customer service skills; younger members teach older members about using social media; both groups compare their respective generation's slang and how the meaning of the word "respect" has evolved over the

years; both groups discuss what sacred texts say about how older and younger people are to treat one another.

4. Older members teach younger members about credit, spending, and saving; younger members teach older members about phone & phishing scams; both groups compare how much things cost now vs. the cost of things in the past and the value of money; both groups discuss what sacred texts say about handling money.

5. Older members teach younger members about proper flag etiquette and what it means to be an American; younger members teach older members photo editing; both groups compare how our country has both changed and remained the same over the years; both groups discuss what sacred texts say about being members of the family of God.

6. Older members teach younger members how to start a campfire, pitch a tent, and/or the outdoor code; younger members teach older members about music streaming and podcasts; both groups compare what it means to care for the environment; both groups discuss what the sacred texts say about our responsibility to care for the earth.

Some best practices to ensure that the class has a lasting impact are to survey participants before and after the class so they can see how their attitudes about the other generation might have changed; pair up older and younger members for long-term co-mentoring and check in calls; and using the participants of the class to form a committee to plan activities that connect generations.

Benefits of Intergenerational Programs:

1. Increased life satisfaction
2. More positive attitudes about aging
3. Increase in functional capacity and reduction in functional limitations of older people
4. Beneficial impact on promoting executive function, memory, and brain activity
5. Older people who regularly participate in activities with children and youth experienced fewer falls, relied less on a cane and demonstrated an increase in social activities
6. Improvement in their self-confidence and feelings about social responsibility amongst younger people

PART 3: CHALLENGE AS OPPORTUNITY

> 7. Reducing involvement in offending behavior and drug use and improving personal resilience.
>
> Alejandro Canedo-García et al., 2021. "Evaluation of the Benefits, Satisfaction, and Limitations of Intergenerational Face-to-Face Activities: A General Population Survey in Spain". *International Journal of Environmental Research and Public Health.* September 14, 2021

A Living History project is a wonderful way for younger members to learn from older members, as well as document and archive the stories of faith builders. Younger members can record interviews with older members and ask questions about their perspectives on living through historical events, personal struggles and how their faith brought them through, as well as lessons they've learned along the way, and include pictures and other mementos before they are lost to time.

Another idea to strengthen intergenerational bonds is through a variety of different service projects that include short-term mission trips, serving meals or clean-up days, packing care packages or assembling gift baskets, nursing home visits, etc. For more ideas, check out the Christian Reformed Church's "25 Ideas for Intergenerational Service". Furthermore, programs such as mentoring, Foster Grandparents, family church camp, family Vacation Bible School, and other similar programs can all be good ideas for intergenerational ministry.

Ideas to Build On

1. Small groups that rotate between members' homes that include people of all ages.
2. Intergenerational book club that read and discuss spiritual books
3. People of all ages participate in different elements of worship
4. Collaborative art and storytelling projects, such as a mural or quilt
5. Collaborative community service projects
6. One-on-one mentoring and/or prayer partnerships
7. Apprenticeships for developing young faith leaders

By implementing intergenerational ministry with purpose and intentionality, faith communities can break out of "separate but equal" generational silos which are so pervasive in churches, synagogues, and the world in general. Stronger connections and social ties between older and younger generations mean healthier faith communities, healthier neighborhoods, and healthier cultures.

Intergenerational Curriculums

1. God's World in Community- available at GenOnMinistries.org
2. LIFT: Living in Faith Together- available at GenOnMinistries.org
3. Current: Seeking Justice Together, Seeking God Together, Seeking Peace Together- available at ShineCurriculum.com/Current
4. Follow Me: Biblical Practices for Faithful Living- available at PCUSAStore.com
5. Intergenerational Learning Programs & Activities- available at IntergenerationalFaith.com
6. LOGOS- available at GenOnMinistries.org

These are just a few of the available curriculums. If you need help deciding which ones are right for your congregation, explore the articles and charts at BuildFaith.org/Choosing-Curriculum

18

Healthy Aging as Ministry

MANY CONGREGATIONS, PARTICULARLY IN communities of color, are recognizing the value in promoting healthy lifestyles as ministry. A 2003 article by Peggy Matteson, PhD RN, cited studies regarding overall health of people involved in faith communities and noted that, "Members of faith groups experience lower rates of heart disease and hypertension, lower rates of cancer, and more satisfaction with their life and their health. When an illness or accident does occur, there is a positive correlation between the odds of survival and the person's degree of religious involvement."[1] *The Lafiya Guide: A Congregational Handbook for Whole-Person Health Ministry* by The Association of Brethren Caregivers further points to the faith foundations of wellness ministry in places of worship "It is out of our response to God's abundant love for us that we can choose to be good stewards of all of our gifts, including our health and wholeness."[2]

> Q. Don't we have doctors for when we get sick? Why do we need health ministry at church? A. Health ministry in the congregation plays an essential role not just in preventing some illnesses but in embodying the gospel's call to live whole and healing lives.
> Church Health Center, Memphis, TN

---

1. See Peggy Matteson, "Health Ministry"
2. See Association of Brethren Caregivers, "Agents of Healing"

There are several models for instituting a health ministry that not only benefits older congregation members, but also those in mid-life and younger who will someday be older adults themselves. The Center for Faith and Community Health Transformation lists nine models currently in use as well as resources for each model which are included in the Resources section of this book:[3]

1. The Health Cabinet Model. The Health Cabinet model integrates health into the life of the faith community. It assumes that all of the activities of the congregation help to promote health–worship, religious education, youth group activities, lay visitation programs, prayer chains, social outreach and action initiatives, etc. The Health Cabinet pulls leaders from all the activities of congregations to plan for how health will be intentionally included in the life of the congregation. It is not a "provider" of health programs, but a partner with other committees and boards to ensure that the health focus is part of all areas of church life. Everyone is part of the healing movement.

2. Mutual Support/Community Building Model. This approach starts with the idea that health is rooted in the quality of people's relationships with one another. Mutual support programs find ways to build community and to facilitate congregational members deepening their relationships with each other. The assumption is that as people share together in meaningful ways about their life experience, those issues that impact a person's overall well-being will be heard and addressed.

3. Faith Community Nursing Model. Faith Community Nursing (formerly Parish Nursing) is a health promotion, disease prevention role based on the care of the whole person and encompassing seven functions–integrator of faith and health, health educator, personal health counselor, referral agent, trainer of volunteers, developer of support groups, and health advocate. This nursing role is a professional model of health ministry using a registered professional nurse. The focus for the practice is the faith community and its ministry.

4. Lay Health Promoters (also known as Community Health Workers or Promotores de Salud) are members of a local congregation or community who are trained in basic health promotion skills. They provide information about health care, monitor those who are chronically ill

---

3. See The Center for Faith and Community Health Transformation, Faith-Based Approaches"

and encourage healthy lifestyles among members of the congregation. They also serve as the "health care connection" between members of their congregation and health care services in the community. This is a practice of listening and teaching. Lay health promoters do not need to have any medical training or background. People who are natural helpers and who are respected by their fellow members are the kind of people who do well in this position.

5. Care and Counseling Model. Many congregations already have strong care and counseling programs. Examples of a program in this model among Christian churches would include Stephen Ministries and Befrienders or Eucharistic Ministers and Ministers of Care. The Jewish tradition of Bikur Cholim mandates visiting the sick and many synagogues have programs that offer this kind of care. In this model, volunteers from the congregation are trained to provide supportive, spiritual care to those in the congregation who are shut-in, experiencing grief or loss, chronically ill, disabled, hospitalized, etc. The model empowers laity to carry out the ministry of the church of healing and comfort to those in need and to bring the symbols of the church to the hurting individual. These powerful ministries offer volunteers an opportunity to grow in their own faith and skills while providing a deep sense of caring and concern within the church.

6. Healing Practices Model. In many congregations clergy and lay leaders practice the laying-on-of-hands or other prayer or liturgical services of healing. Most faiths have some kind of healing tradition that is part of their practice. In other congregations, interested members may receive training in various healing techniques—massage therapy, meditation, guided imagery, Reiki, healing touch, movement or art therapy, etc.—and offer healing sessions for members of the congregation and community.

7. Coalition Model. Some projects work through coalitions of congregations and community organizations that come together around particular needs. The group may choose to serve the whole community, or just focus on a specific health topic, such as the terminally ill, older adults, people with HIV/AIDS, families with children with disabilities, people with chronic illness, etc. Coalition approaches can look very different depending on the particular mix of partners. Some may utilize volunteers to provide a set of services such as transportation,

yard work, home repair, childcare, meal preparation, etc. Others may become politically active and work for legislative change or to change the way in which services are provided. Some may focus on community-wide education events, health fairs, or other health promotion activities.

8. Public Health and Faith Collaborations Model. Many departments of public health around the country have already identified the faith community as an important partner in health promotion and are actively working with churches, mosques, synagogues and temples to eliminate health disparities. However, congregations need to take care to go beyond simply holding health fairs or opening their space for programs. Congregations can also take leadership in shaping initiatives that are faith-based and that engage the congregation in ministry.

9. Health Centers Model. Some congregations choose to actually provide health services in their building. Or they may come together with other congregations to create a health clinic in their neighborhood or in another community that has health needs.

Why Congregational Health Ministry?

1. Health is for the whole person. God loves the whole person. Congregations can assist with change in all the dimensions of life that impact health—emotional, nutrition, movement, medical and work, along with the more obvious areas of faith and friendship.

2. Healing ministry is love in action. Congregational health ministry puts action on the words we believe—that we are beloved by God, that God offers us an abundant life, that Jesus healed both body and spirit. Building on the assets already present in their midst, congregations can motivate people in ways most health-minded programs cannot touch. Health ministry is a natural fit in a faith community, in everything from blood pressure clinics, cooking classes, exercise groups, social gatherings, and support groups to having a faith community nurse as a paid member of the staff.

3. Churches hold many of the ingredients of healing. Health ministry is an organized effort to address health and wellness needs in the congregation, but it can take many forms. Worshipers see each other regularly. All ages participate. Social support is available. Volunteers are ready to help. They

influence the surrounding community. They reach out to those in need—including need for healing. All these factors contribute to health.

4. Health ministry makes a difference. Both individuals and the congregation as a whole benefit from health ministry. As the congregation journeys to find wholeness and well-being as individuals, they discover that together they are better prepared to reach out and serve the community around them.

Church Health Center, Memphis, TN ChurchHealth.org

Another tool for shaping a health ministry is the Substance Abuse and Mental Health Services Administration's Eight Dimensions of Wellness. The Eight Dimensions of Wellness can be used in conjunction with an existing model like one of the ones mentioned above, or it can just be treated as a lens through which health-promotion activities should be considered, as they encompass a whole person's health and well-being. The Eight Dimensions of Wellness may also be a helpful tool in determining inclusive older adult programming as mentioned in Chapter 12 of this book. The Eight Dimensions of Wellness include:

1. Physical- incorporates nutrition, physical activity, sleep, substance use, medication safety, and preventative medicine. Examples include exercise classes, nutrition and cooking classes, medication management and other wellness seminar topics, fall prevention seminars, vaccine clinics, etc.

2. Intellectual- incorporates personal interests, education, brain exercises, and conversations. Examples include art, music or hobby classes, seminars on topics of interest, outings to museums, technology classes, etc.

3. Financial- incorporates income, spending and saving, debt, and investing. Examples include MoneySmart (available for free through the FDIC), seminars on Medicare and retirement investment products, Financial Peace University, tax clinic, etc.

4. Environmental- incorporates accessing clean air, food, and water; preserving the areas where we live, learn, and work; occupying pleasant, stimulating environments that support our well-being; and promoting learning, contemplation, and relaxation in natural places and spaces. Examples include hiking groups, neighborhood clean-ups, gardening classes, etc.

5. Spiritual- incorporates one's personal beliefs and values and involves having meaning, purpose, and a sense of balance and peace. Examples include worship services, study of sacred texts, hymns and spiritual songs, prayer groups, etc.
6. Social- incorporates healthy relationships with friends, family, and the community, and having an interest in and concern for the needs of others and humankind. Examples include luncheons, game days, group outings, etc.
7. Occupational- activities that provide meaning and purpose and reflect personal values, interests, and beliefs, including employment. Examples include service projects, committees, volunteering, etc.
8. Emotional- incorporates feelings and emotions, self-care, and stress. Examples include support groups, pastoral counseling, stress management classes, etc.

There are several great reasons for incorporating a health ministry in your community of faith. The first is that health ministry gives congregation members the tools needed to age well, instead of just growing older, which can lead to better health outcomes and more independence in later life. The second is that health ministry can easily be intergenerational, which further strengthens the overall health of the congregation by making more connection points between members. The third reason is that health ministry serves the whole person- mind, body, and spirit- which can help deepen an individual's personal faith by showing them that God is at work in every aspect of their lives.

> The Link Between Faith and Public Health. A 2018 study of African-American faith communities revealed that while most of them had some form of health ministry, they were not connected to evidence-based interventions that have been developed by research. While researchers are great at identifying and testing which programs work best, they are not great at disseminating that information. Faith communities are the perfect place for those programs to work, but they are not great at knowing how to access those interventions. By working together with public health agencies and universities, congregations can reap the benefits of the research.

Part 3: Challenge as Opportunity

The Eight Dimensions Of Wellness

Physical– Recognizing the need for physical activity, nutrition, and sleep

Intellectual– Recognizing creative abilities and finding ways to expand knowledge and skills.

Financial– Satisfaction with current and future financial situations

Environmental– Good health by occupying pleasant, stimulating environments that support well-being

Spiritual– Expanding our sense of purpose and meaning in life

Social– Developing a sense of connection, belonging, and a well-developed support system

Occupational– Personal satisfaction and enrichment derived from one's work

Emotional– Coping effectively with life and creating satisfying relationships

19

Conducting a Needs Assessment

FROM TIME TO TIME, it is necessary for faith communities to take stock of the health of their congregations and assess which needs should be addressed and how they should be prioritized. Some of the available literature suggested an annual assessment, others, like the Roman Catholic Diocese of Rochester suggested it be "done every five years in order to assess the value of a parish's current ministries and to, perhaps, uncover unmet needs in the community where a new ministry might add value".[1]

Conducting a faith community health survey that assesses the overall health and adherence to mission, values, and goals is certainly very useful and there are several professional tools available which are listed in the resources section of this book. However, since this book focuses solely on the needs of older adult members, the surveys in this chapter are directed towards them more generally. It can help identify areas of strengths and weaknesses, as well as identify potential volunteers and program leaders (or lack thereof).

> "Meeting the needs of a community is not a one-time act but a continuous process that requires ongoing assessment and adaptation. As communities evolve, their needs can change, and what worked once may not be effective anymore. Churches need to stay

1. See Roman Catholic Diocese of Rochester, "Conducting a Community Needs Assessment"

attuned to these changes and be willing to adjust their strategies accordingly." BibleChat.ai

It may be difficult to get members on board with taking a survey, because many may feel that it opens the door for negative church/synagogue politics, or they may fear some kind of retribution for their answers. Some members may be apathetic or feel as if their opinion doesn't matter. The Arkansas Baptists State Convention recommends that "Pastors should also assure people that the results of the assessment will not be used as a means of pushing a pre-determined agenda, attacking someone's ministry, or pointing guilt and blame at people in the church. People should be reminded that an assessment is a way of getting the most feedback from as many members as possible and that is a way of valuing everyone's perspective."[2] Programs that really take root and do good work are those that members feel a vested interest in, and vested interest can be created by really taking the time to make people feel valued and heard.

Ideally, the survey should be conducted anonymously to allow older members to freely express their needs and ideas without fear of being judged. Once the survey results are processed, the next step might be to conduct open forums where members can voice their concerns and opinions, as well as bounce ideas off each other. The next logical step would be to create a plan of action, and then finally execute the plan. To make the survey as accessible as possible, it is recommended that it be distributed via both email and hardcopy. Don't be surprised if you only receive a relatively low response on your survey; a low response rate doesn't necessarily mean the survey was a failure, but it may indicate a need for better explanation and buy-in from members of the congregation. It may be helpful for an announcement to be made 2–3 weeks in a row that the survey will be coming out and its intended purpose, as well as announcements in bulletins, newsletters and emails. That gives a bigger impression of the importance of the survey and gives members the chance to think about how they might respond to the questions.

The How & Why of a Needs Assessment

1. Understand the Community. The first step in effectively serving the community is understanding its unique needs and challenges. This requires a commitment to building

2. See Arkansas Baptists State Convention, "Conducting a Church Assessment"

Conducting a Needs Assessment

relationships with community members and engaging in active listening.
2. Spiritual Integration. While practical help is crucial, the church's unique contribution to community service also includes spiritual support. This means not only addressing physical needs but also providing pastoral care, prayer, and opportunities for spiritual growth. Many people in distress are seeking not just material but also spiritual solace.

BibleChat.ai. "How can churches effectively assess and meet the needs of their local community?"

Gauging the overall health and experiences of older members can also help faith communities identify trends in the broader scope of aging and particular needs in each area. This information can then be shared with local government leaders to enact policy changes and possible interventions; faith communities are very well-placed in this situation because people are generally more trusting of a survey that comes from a place of faith rather than from the government, and because faith communities can have a unique influence in local government.

The results of the needs assessment can also direct leadership as to which issues are the most critical so that efforts can be focused on addressing those needs first. Depending on the results of the survey and the needs to be addressed, it may be necessary to collaborate with denominational leadership or even other faith communities in your local area.

The following pages contain two different surveys that can be used for your congregation. The first model is based on the challenges that older adults face as outlined in the earlier chapters of this book. The second model is a questionnaire patterned after the Midsouth Congregational Health Needs Assessments[3]. These surveys can be given all at one time, or they can be given out one section at a time if the entire thing seems too intimidating. The next chapter delves more deeply into analyzing the survey data and the steps needed to turn thoughts and ideas into actions.

---

3. See "Mid-South Congregational Health Needs Assessment"

PART 3: CHALLENGE AS OPPORTUNITY

Older Adults Survey

Thank you for taking this survey! Your honest feedback is very important to us so that we can understand how to serve you better. Helping us to understand what challenges you face is the first step in building a faith home that serves all people. We invite you to share your thoughts, opinions, and ideas on what needs to be improved. This survey is anonymous, and the results will be used to improve our building, worship services, and programs.

Please circle your responses.

Have you had a fall in the past year?   Yes   No

Are you worried about experiencing a fall?   Yes   No

How would you rate the accessibility of our building?

Very Accessible   Somewhat Accessible   Neutral   Not Accessible

What areas of the building are most difficult for you to navigate? Circle all that apply:

Parking lot	Exterior doors	Bathroom stalls
Sidewalks	Interior doors	Bathroom sinks
Curbs	Signs	Pews
Flooring	Hallways	Seats

What other areas are difficult for you to navigate? How would you improve these areas?

_____
_____
_____
_____
_____
_____

Conducting a Needs Assessment

Are you or is someone close to you experiencing memory loss?   Yes   No

How concerned are you about getting dementia?
Very Concerned   Somewhat Concerned   Neutral   Not Concerned

If you had dementia, would you want there to be programs and practices that made it easier for you to still be involved in worship?   Yes   No

If you had dementia, or had to care for someone with dementia, do you feel as though you would be supported and included?   Yes   No   Neutral

How good of a job are we currently doing for those members who have dementia?
Great Job   Good Job   Neutral   Bad Job   Not Doing Anything

What practices, programs, or policies would help us do a better job at caring for people with dementia? _____
_____
_____
_____
_____
_____

Do you have problems with your eyesight?   Yes   No   Sometimes

Do you feel comfortable driving at night?   Yes   No   Sometimes

Do you have difficulty seeing or reading our signs, bulletins, posters, and other printed materials?   Yes   No   Sometimes

Do you have problems with your hearing?   Yes   No   Sometimes

Part 3: Challenge as Opportunity

Are you able to clearly hear during worship services?   Yes   No   Sometimes

What kinds of things would help you feel more comfortable seeing and hearing clearly?

_____
_____
_____
_____
_____
_____

How often do you feel lonely or isolated?
Very Often   Sometimes   Neutral   Rarely   Never

How big of a problem is loneliness and isolation for older adults?
Huge Problem   Big Problem   Neutral   Small Problem   No Problem

If you were not able to leave your home, do you feel as though you would feel supported and included by our congregation?   Yes   No   Neutral

How good of a job are we currently doing for those members who are lonely, isolated, or shut-in?
Great Job   Good Job   Neutral   Bad Job   Not Doing Anything

What practices, programs, or policies would help us do a better job at caring for people who are lonely, isolated or shut-in? _____

_____
_____
_____
_____
_____
_____
_____
_____

Conducting a Needs Assessment

Are you currently caring for the everyday needs of a parent, spouse, child, grandchild, neighbor, friend, or loved one?   Yes   No   Sometimes

Do you feel as though caring for your loved one is taking over your life?
Yes   No   Sometimes

How concerned are you about your ability to continue to care for your loved one?
Very concerned   Somewhat concerned   Neutral   Not concerned

What kinds of things do you worry most about as a caregiver? Circle all that apply:

Finances	Physically Wearing Out	Emotions
Not Able to Work	Mentally Wearing Out	Not Enough Food
Too Much to Do	Not Enough Help	Transportation
No Time for Self-Care	Feeling Burnt Out	Feeling Forgotten

Other:_____

If you are caring for someone else's daily needs, how often do you feel included and supported in your role by our congregation?
Always   Sometimes   Neutral   Rarely   Never

What are your thoughts and ideas about how we could better care for caregivers?

_____
_____
_____
_____
_____
_____
_____
_____

Part 3: Challenge as Opportunity

Have you ever been the victim of elder abuse, fraud, or a scam?
Yes   No   I'm Not Sure

How worried are you about elder abuse, fraud, and scams?
Very worried   Somewhat Worried   Neutral   Not Worried

If you were to be the victim of elder abuse, fraud, or a scam, would you feel safe enough to tell someone here?   Yes   No   Maybe

If you were the victim of elder abuse, fraud, or a scam, would you want someone here to help you report it?   Yes   No   Maybe

What practices, programs, or policies would help us do a better job at caring for people who have been a victim and/or preventing elder abuse, fraud, and scams?
_____
_____
_____
_____
_____
_____
_____

Do you have problems getting along with your children and family?
Yes   No   Sometimes   Don't Have Any Family

Do you feel that pastoral counseling might help with some of the problems between you and your family?   Yes   No   Maybe

Do you feel that you are struggling with grief?   Yes   No   Maybe

Conducting a Needs Assessment

Do you feel that you could use some help with your emotional health?
Yes   No   Maybe

Would you be interested in joining a support group?
Yes   No   Maybe

What are your thoughts and opinions about how we can better serve those who are grieving, have family issues, or who need emotional support?
_____
_____
_____
_____
_____
_____

Do you sometimes run out of food before the end of the month?
Yes   No   Sometimes

Do you have difficulty getting to the grocery store, shopping, and/or transporting groceries home?   Yes   No   Sometimes

Do you have concerns about your ability to pay rent and utilities?
Yes   No   Sometimes

Do you have concerns about how long you'll be able to safely live at home?
Yes   No   Sometimes

Are you still able to drive, or do you have reliable transportation?
Yes   No   Sometimes

Do you feel safe in your neighborhood?   Yes   No   Sometimes

Part 3: Challenge as Opportunity

Is your neighborhood clean and well-kept, or is it trashy and overgrown?
    Clean   Trashy   Neutral

What practices, programs, or policies would help us do a better job at caring for people who are struggling with having enough food, a safe place to live, and adequate transportation?

_____
_____
_____
_____
_____

Are you able to walk (or use a wheelchair or scooter) around your neighborhood?
    Yes   No   Neutral

Do you have a convenient place to exercise?   Yes   No

What health concerns do you have? Circle all that apply:

High Blood Pressure	Diabetes	Arthritis
High Cholesterol	Kidney Disease	Dementia
Heart Disease	Asthma/COPD	

Other:_____

If we were to offer health, wellness, and exercise programs, how likely would you be to participate?
    Very Likely   Somewhat Likely   Neutral   Not Likely

What are your thoughts and opinions about how we can better serve those who have concerns about their health?

_____
_____
_____
_____
_____

Conducting a Needs Assessment

How connected do you feel to younger people in our congregation?
Very Connected   Somewhat Connected   Neutral   Not Connected

How interested are you in connecting with younger people?
Very Interested   Somewhat Interested   Neutral   Not Interested

What kinds of ministry or volunteer opportunities would you be interested in? Circle all that apply:

Children's Ministries	Caregiver Respite	Food Programs
Adult Education	Dementia Programs	Clothes Closet
Music Ministry	Evangelism	Prayer Warrior
Visiting Shut Ins	Bus Driver/Carpool	Wellness Programs
Local Outreach	Missions	Cards & Calls

Other:_____

PART 3: CHALLENGE AS OPPORTUNITY

Congregational Health Needs Survey

Questions About You
INSTRUCTIONS: Please respond to each question to the best of your ability. Please DO NOT put your name on the form.

1. What is your age? _____ (years)

2. What is your gender? (Check one)
Male
Female
Prefer not to respond

3. What is your race/ethnicity? (Check one)
Black/African American
Hispanic/Latino
White
Asian American/Pacific Islander
American Indian/Alaskan Native
Multiracial
Other
Prefer not to respond

4. What is your marital status? (Check one)
Single
Married or in a committed relationship
Divorced or separated
Widowed
Prefer not to respond

5. What best describes your educational level? (Check one)
Less than High School
High School diploma (or have GED)
Some college credit, but no degree
Two-year degree (e.g., technical, Associate's)
Four-year degree (i.e., Bachelor's)
Graduate or professional degree (e.g., Master's, doctorate, MD, DDS, PharmD)
Prefer not to respond

Conducting a Needs Assessment

6. What is your main role at your church? (That is, what role do you spend most of your time performing?) (Check one)
Pastor/Pastor's Spouse
Associate Pastor/Other Minister
Non-Clergy Staff
Non-Staff Volunteer Leader
Member/Regular Attendee
Health Ministry Leader/Member
Parish/Faith Community Nurse
Prefer not to respond

7. I have been a member/have been attending my congregation for: (Check one)
Less than a year
1 year – 5 years
Over 5 years
Prefer not to respond

8. What is the main reason that you attend your congregation? (Check one)
The Spirit
Tradition
Preaching
Prayer
Music/Singing
Scriptural study
Friends
Support from others
Different ministries offered
Prefer not to respond

9. When life gets hard, I find strength and support from: (Check ALL that apply)
Congregation
Congregational leader/Pastor
Congregation members
Family & friends
Prayer and Meditation
Other
Specify:
Prefer not to respond

Part 3: Challenge as Opportunity

Questions About Your Congregation

INSTRUCTIONS: Please respond to each question to the best of your ability. Please DO NOT put your name on the form.

10. Are health topics important to your pastor? (Check one)
Yes
No
I don't know/I don't remember
Prefer not to respond

11. Does your church have any of the following? (Check ALL that apply)
Health Ministry/Wellness Ministry
Health Fairs
Guest Health Speakers/Health Education Classes
Flyers About Health Resources in the Community
Health Screenings or a Health Clinic
Navigation/Referral to Health Services
Community Partners
Partnerships with other Churches/Faith-Based Organizations
Prefer not to respond

12. Do you want to expand or further develop your church's approach(es) to health? (Check one)
Yes
No
Prefer not to respond

Conducting a Needs Assessment

MIND, BODY, AND SOUL   Place an X next to ALL the concerns that apply to you
Anxiety or Depression
Asthma/Breathing problems
Cancer
Caregiving
Chronic pain
Dental/Oral care
Diabetes/High sugar levels
Eating Disorders
Falls
Heart Disease (e.g., heart attack, high cholesterol)
High Blood Pressure or Stroke
HIV/AIDS and Sexually transmitted diseases
Loneliness / Social Isolation
Memory (e.g., Dementia, Alzheimer)
Nutrition or Physical activity
Overweight / Obesity
Smoking/Tobacco use
Stress
Substance Abuse/Addiction
Suicide
Teen pregnancy
Trauma (e.g., domestic abuse, crime victim, childhood adverse events)
Other:

AVAILABILITY OF RESOURCES
Affordable Healthcare/Healthcare information
Childcare
Employment/Jobs
Financial Assistance
Healthy Foods
Health Services (e.g., screenings, doctors, clinics, caregivers, prenatal care)
Mental Health / Substance Abuse Clinics
Programs for Youth
Programs for Seniors
Quality Education
Recreation Centers and Facilities
Respite / Adult Day Care
Transportation

Part 3: Challenge as Opportunity

Across the three sections, select the TOP NEEDS you would like your church/congregation to address with future programming (Check 3 Needs)

MIND, BODY, AND SOUL
Anxiety or Depression
Asthma/Breathing problems
Cancer
Caregiving
Chronic pain
Dental/Oral care
Diabetes/High sugar levels
Eating Disorders
Falls
Heart Disease (e.g., heart attack, high cholesterol)
High Blood Pressure or Stroke
HIV/AIDS and Sexually transmitted diseases
Loneliness / Social Isolation
Memory (e.g., Dementia, Alzheimer)
Nutrition or Physical activity
Overweight / Obesity
Smoking/Tobacco use
Stress
Substance Abuse/Addiction
Suicide
Teen pregnancy
Trauma (e.g., domestic abuse, crime victim, childhood adverse events)
Other:

AVAILABILITY OF RESOURCES
Affordable Healthcare/Healthcare information
Childcare
Employment/Jobs
Financial Assistance
Healthy Foods
Health Services (e.g., screenings, doctors, clinics, caregivers, prenatal care)
Mental Health / Substance Abuse Clinics
Programs for Youth
Programs for Seniors
Quality Education
Recreation Centers and Facilities
Respite / Adult Day Care
Transportation

Conducting a Needs Assessment

NEIGHBORHOOD ISSUES
Crime/Assault/Homicide
Discrimination/Racism
Domestic Violence
Drug Use
Homelessness
Incarceration/Re-entry into the community
Police Behaviors/Practices
Safe and Affordable Housing
Sanitation (e.g., rats, trash)/Vacant Houses

In your opinion, what are the important barriers to addressing the NEEDS you selected above? (Mark ALL that apply)
Not a priority
Lack of funds
Need for training
Need for committed staff
Limited time
Physical space limitations
Need help from outside the church
Need being met outside of church
Other: Specify _____

20

Analyzing Results & Effecting Changes

CONDUCTING A NEEDS ASSESSMENT is only one step in effecting changes in your place of worship. It opens the door for conversations about issues such as safe neighborhoods, lack of accessibility in your building, food insecurity, how to better serve certain members, etc. Some of what comes to light may already be old news, and some of it may come as a surprise because the human tendency is to hide problems and present the façade that everything is ok. A needs assessment will also most likely open doors to conversations about your faith community's budget and capacity to fill the gaps identified by the assessment.

> "For any community project to maintain credibility and effectiveness, it must operate with transparency and accountability. This involves clear communication with both church members and the wider community about the goals, processes, and outcomes of community projects. Financial transparency is particularly important, as it builds trust and ensures that resources are used effectively." BibleChat.ai

There are a few steps involved in analyzing what needs to be done, how and when it needs to be done, who will be in charge, how much it will cost, and how you will measure success. If done too hastily, the changes could end up causing more problems than they solve. So what is the first step?

Analyzing Results & Effecting Changes

The first step is to sit down with your leaders and discuss what gaps they've seen or heard about from congregation members and staff. This is just a brainstorming session, a starting point. As a leadership group, discuss what kind of broad vision or outcome you hope to see happen before sending out a needs survey to get their input on what is working well and what isn't. It would be helpful to have data from outside sources, such as your denomination, your city/county government, etc. to help gain a clearer image of the needs and gaps in your community. Here are some questions to keep in mind:

1. What needs are we trying to solve?
2. Are we trying to solve a certain problem, or a process?
3. What processes are already in place?
4. What kinds of barriers might we encounter?
5. What kind of outcomes are we looking for?
6. Are we adhering to our mission and values?
7. What timeframe should we use to make changes?
8. What is our budget and what resources do we have available?
9. Are other faith communities in our area struggling with the same issues?

Another brainstorming method you could use is the S.W.O.T analysis. Identify your faith community's Strengths, Weaknesses, Opportunities, and Threats. An example of this analysis can be found in the Roman Catholic Archdiocese of Atlanta Pastoral Plan:[1]

1. Strengths are internal, positive attributes, capabilities or resources that distinguish one parish from another. They can include experience, knowledge, quality of the work, reputation, unique skills of the leadership team or ministries or parishioners.
2. Weaknesses are internal factors within your control that may inhibit your ability to achieve your objectives. They could include a lack of skills, staffing issues, leadership, motivation, competition from other churches or financial or physical resources.

---

1. See Roman Catholic Archdiocese of Atlanta Pastoral Plan, "Parish Needs Assessment"

PART 3: CHALLENGE AS OPPORTUNITY

3. Opportunities are external factors or conditions that can lead to improvement, growth, addition of resources or solutions to nagging problems or conditions. They could include training, recruitment of new talent, additional funding, synergies with other parishes or diocesan support, growth of new ministries.

4. Threats are real, tangible, internal or external issues that could jeopardize the parish's mission or performance. They could include a decline in membership, decline in collections, loss of program funding, loss of key leaders, competition from other non-Catholic churches, natural disasters involving the physical resources, changes in political or social fabric of the community

> The How and Why of a Needs Assessment Continued.
>
> 1. No church exists in isolation. Every community has a network of organizations, schools, businesses, and other churches. Effective community service involves forming partnerships with these entities. Collaborative efforts can lead to a greater pool of resources, shared responsibilities, and a broader impact than any single organization could achieve alone.
>
> 2. Effective community service is not just about meeting external needs but also about empowering the community itself. This involves identifying and nurturing local leaders who understand their community's challenges and have the trust and respect of their peers. Churches can support these leaders by providing training, resources, and opportunities to lead initiatives.
>
> BibleChat.ai. How can churches effectively assess and meet the needs of their local community?

Once you've gathered your information from outside sources and your leadership brainstorming session(s), then prepare your older adults for the survey. It may have to be explained to them a few times and in different ways for them to buy into what it is you are trying to do. Try approaching them in their Sunday School or group meetings, as well as via newsletters, bulletins, flyers, and email. Don't forget to include those older adults that haven't been to church in a while; you may need to call them on the phone and explain why their help in answering the survey is needed. Have a firm date for when the surveys should be completed, and be sure to reiterate the deadline for having the survey turned in. To help with anonymity, a drop box can be placed in a centrally located area of the building, or the surveys can be returned by mail or email. If there is concern about the length of the survey or the faith institution's ability to effect change, it is entirely possible to only give members one section of the survey at a time and then work towards fixing those issues first.

Once the surveys have been returned, the next step is to analyze the data. Depending on how many surveys need to be analyzed, it might be helpful to number each survey and then use a spreadsheet to track the answers. Numbering each survey also helps to track the open-ended responses so that they can be referenced again later. This is what a spreadsheet might look like:

Older Adults Survey
Fall Prevention Section

#	Had a Fall	Worried About A fall	Access Rating	Parking Lot	Side-walk	Curb	Floor	Ex Doors	Int Doors	Signs	Halls	Bath Stalls	Bath Sinks	Pews	Seats
1	X	X	Somewhat	X	X	X	X	X	X	X	X	X	X	X	X
2		X	Very					X	X				X		
3	X		Neutral												
4	X	X	Not Access	X		X		X			X		X		
5			Very												
6		X	Somewhat							X					
7			Very	X	X	X	X	X	X	X	X	X	X	X	X
8	X		Neutral		X	X		X	X		X	X		X	X
9		X	Very												
10			Neutral												

Don't worry if there seems to be conflicting data or trends that don't make sense; the survey is asking people questions about their perceptions which can change depending on the lens through which they view the question. There are also cases where the questions are misread or misinterpreted. In the example spreadsheet, one respondent perceived the building as being "somewhat accessible", but marked every single area of concern, whereas another respondent marked neutral and no areas of concern. One respondent perceived the building as being inaccessible but only marked a few areas of concern; whereas another respondent perceived the building as being very accessible but still marked every area of concern. Even though the data seems somewhat contradictory at first glance, it is still possible to see trends emerging- in this example, half of the respondents were worried about having a fall and the problem areas most identified were exterior doors and pews. The second most areas of concern were curbs, interior doors, bathroom stalls, and signs. Now leadership has something to work with, and plans can begin to be formed.

The next step in the process is to have focus groups of older adult members (and in some cases, caregivers and other interested parties) to discuss the results of the survey and their ideas for what changes need to be made. It may be necessary to also address with the group budgetary constraints and the need to think of creative solutions. The members may have some unique solutions or be able to recommend a certain company or person. The focus groups can also identify who is willing and able to volunteer to make the changes happen. For example, the sample survey identified key areas of concern for members, such as exterior doors, curbs, signs, etc. Now is the time to drill down and find out exactly what the problems are with those areas of concern and how to fix them. For some, the exterior doors might have been identified as a problem because they are too heavy, shut too quickly, or are too difficult to open while using a walker or wheelchair. Then the solutions could be either adjusting the closing mechanisms or installing an automatic opening device. A focus group member may pop up and state that their nephew works for a company that installs handicapped accessible doors, so now leadership has an inroad to getting a cost estimate.

The next step would be to regroup with leadership and discuss the results of the survey and the ideas brought forth at the focus groups to see where the highest priority needs are. In the above example survey result, the greatest areas of concern were clearly identified, and then ideas for how to rework those areas were pitched and brainstormed during the focus group phase. Now leadership has more clearly defined goals to achieve and it becomes a matter of deciding which solutions work best with the budget, time constraints, mission and values, etc. This is also a good time to assign tasks and timelines and gather volunteers. It will be necessary for leadership to meet periodically for updates on the progress of changes being made, and it will also be necessary to get feedback on how well the changes are working or if they need to be tweaked.

S.M.A.R.T. Goals

1. Specific: Be specific about who is involved or responsible for accomplishing the goal.

Analyzing Results & Effecting Changes

2. Measurable: Include wording that will measure the progress your congregation is making towards their goal. How much? How many? How will you know when you reach your goal?
3. Actionable: Your congregation can attain most any goal you set if tangible steps can be taken towards achieving that goal.
4. Realistic: To be realistic, a goal must be one your congregation is willing and able to do.
5. Time Sensitive: A goal should have a specific time frame. For these goals, make them something you can achieve over the next year.

There is another method called S.M.A.R.T. Goals that can be used to analyze your survey data that is recommended by the Midsouth Congregational Health Needs Assessment team. Includedon the following page is a worksheet to help manage your goals and keep your leadership team on task:

Effecting changes in your building's design and in your program delivery takes time and patience, and a best practice is to focus on one section at a time. Effecting change also requires both empathy and a thick skin; it is inevitable that making changes may cause some people to criticize. However, behaviors are often driven by emotions or an unmet need- if one were to peel back the layers and ask more questions as to why that critical person feels the way they do, it could perhaps build a bridge of understanding rather than fester a sore spot. Keep in mind the whys of effecting changes- to meet the unmet needs to those who are often overlooked in the congregation, to strengthen the health of the congregation, and most importantly, to serve God.

Part 3: Challenge as Opportunity

Goal & Action Plan # ___ for Your Congregation Health Needs

1. What is the congregational need you wish to address in the next [fill in a time period that is no longer than one year]?

2a. What SMART goal(s) will help you address this need? Include as many goals as necessary to address the identified need.

2b. Specific objectives, timeline and milestones, and relevancy. Repeat this step for each SMART goal identified in 2a.

Goal:			
What are the specific objectives for each goal? (define)	What is the timeline and milestones for these objectives? (include dates)	What is the relevancy of the objective to the goal?	Who is responsible for this objective?

2c. How will you know your goal has been achieved? Repeat this step for each SMART goal. Goal:
Goal Milestone:
Completion date:

3a. How will you hold this team and the church accountable for achieving this goal? Repeat this step for each SMART goal.

3b. What steps will you take to celebrate the completion of a milestone?

3c. How will you recognize those who helped the church achieve the milestone?

3d. What steps will you take if you miss a milestone?

4. How will you communicate success? How will you communicate changes?

Analyzing Results & Effecting Changes

10 Keys to Leading Change in a Church.

1. No Change Is Perfectly Executed. No matter how well-planned change is, how good it looks on paper, or how much sense it makes in your head, it's not going to go the way you think it's going to go.
2. Communication Is Key. During change management, communicating the right message to the right audience at the right time is essential and can take a lot of time.
3. Everyone Carries Two Buckets. Everyone carries around two buckets with them: a bucket of water and a bucket of gasoline. One fuels change, and the other puts it out. Water fuels change because it douses the fire of resistance. Gasoline puts change out because it fuels the fire of resistance.
4. Think Ahead. Most people are fine with change as long as it doesn't affect them.
5. It Isn't Easy. Change is hard, it takes time, and requires grit and courage.
6. The Ripple Effect. Change has a ripple effect that often goes unseen until much later.
7. The Minority Tend to Have a Majority Voice. In a season of change, a small group of people can have a loud voice and make it seem like everyone is against you.
8. Lead Differently with Different People. Anyone who has more than one kid knows you don't parent every kid identically. In the same way, don't try to lead every group through change the same way.
9. Small Changes Can Reveal Big Issues. One small, seemingly harmless change can tell you something about your church.
10. Training vs. Challenging. Sometimes people don't have the right information and don't understand why they should get on board with the change. Other times people don't want to jump on board with the change because they have their own agenda.

Paul Alexander, 2024. "10 Keys to Leading Change in a Church", The Unstuck Group. TheUnstuckGroup.com

21

Member Retention

OVER THE LAST TWO decades, research has indicated that overall attendance at religious services is declining, and additional research on pre- and post-pandemic attendance indicates an even faster rate of decline. Here are some facts and figures about religious service attendance:

1. According to the 2022 American Religious Benchmark Survey, "Before the pandemic, 75 percent of Americans reported attending religious services at least monthly. By spring 2022, that figure dropped to 68 percent attending at least monthly."[1]

2. The 2022 American Religious Benchmark Survey also indicated that 16% of people ages 65 and older attend religious services less than they did pre-pandemic.

3. A Gallup study compared rates of religious attendance from 2000 to 2023 and concluded that, "On any given weekend, about three in 10 U.S. adults attend religious services, down from 42% two decades ago."[2]

---

[1]. See David Roach, "Church Attendance Dropped Among Young People, Singles, Liberals"

[2]. See Jeffery M Jones, "Church Attendance Has Declined in Most U.S. Religious Groups"

4. Research from the Institute for Family Studies indicated that, "Perhaps unsurprisingly due to increased health risks, adults who are 65 and older are much less likely to attend at least monthly now (32%) than before the pandemic (41%)"[3]

5. Only 30% of Protestant Christians and 16% of Jews attend weekly worship services. Gallup.com

It's not surprising that the Covid-19 pandemic has had a lasting impact on the faith community; concerns for public health and safety had places of worship closing their doors, often for months. However, what may come as a surprise is why many older adults have not returned to the church or synagogue, or why they are exiting now. For a long time, older adults have been the backbone of the ones filling up the pews. It has been generally accepted that younger people who were raised in a faith community often drop out of attendance but then make a return in adulthood when they are ready to settle down and raise a family, and then remain in the faith community until they are old. However, as the song goes, "the times they are a-changin'".

An article in *Christianity Today* cited a survey from the Pew Research Center that indicated, "Among those over 65 who didn't attend church, 45 percent said they don't go to church because "I practice my faith in other ways." About the same proportion of people between 50 and 64 said the same. In other words, just under half of Christians over 40 who stop attending church feel they're still practicing their faith."[4] It seems that one reason older adults stop attending religious services is that they no longer see the value in it. The article interviewed Pastor Nate Phillips of Kirk in the Hills Presbyterian Church in Michigan who relayed a conversation with a member who stopped attending: "I love you. I love the people there," the man explained. "But quite frankly, I'm getting everything I get at church in my soccer club." The article further pointed out that "people who perceive church as a place to hear uplifting sermons or to get moral calibration might point out the convenience of listening to recorded messages and songs. Such activities might be why many older church dropouts believe they are still practicing their faith, still learning, still worshiping".Rabbi Richard Address of SacredAging.com reflected the trend in an interview

---

3. See Aaron Earles, "5 Current Church Attendance Trends You Need to Know"
4. See Adam MacInnis, "The Church Is Losing Its Gray Heads"

for this book and stated that nearly half of Jews over age 50 are leaving the synagogue because they feel there is nothing for them there.

Another reason why older adults leave the church is because they don't feel valued themselves. In an interview for this book, Bishop Kenneth Carder of the United Methodist Church was noted as saying, "Churches see older adults as a liability; I'd like to see churches see them as an asset...Our society is rooted in individualism, our worth is based on our capacities. The church gives us the perspective that we are created, and of belonging. Churches are uniquely positioned to create communities for aging based on the concept of love, acceptance, and belonging rather than on one's abilities or capacities." The same sentiment is reflected in the article from *Christianity Today*: "Are you making sure that your older generations have a place in your church? I think the fact that they have been faithful church attenders their whole life and now they're walking away from church in their 50s and 60s really says something that they're feeling very deeply about belonging or value."

A third reason why older adults leave the church is due to major life events, such as moving, an empty nest, or a health issue. For older adults experiencing a major life event, the act of going to religious services may be too much of a hassle, the benefit of going may not be enough to outweigh the effort to get there, their friends may have left, or they may not feel supported enough in their new stage of life.

Other Reasons Boomers Leave the Church

1. Churches have changed worship to the point that older generations now feel out of place and ill-prepared to keep up. Everyone wants a church filled with energetic, enthusiastic young people, but they don't want to attend a service that feels like a youth group for adults.
2. Our culture has changed so rapidly, and churches are reactive rather than proactive in negotiating these changes. The prevailing feeling is that an encroaching culture of change in the digital age has dumbed down faith.
3. Seasoned saints no longer attend church because they are busy like everyone else. This has to do with the changing landscape of family life and split families.

Joe LaGuardia, 2015. "3 Reasons People Over 60 Leave Your Church". GoodFaithMedia.org

Member Retention

So what is the key to retaining older congregation members? The key is to make communities of faith spaces where older adults feel treasured, heard, and needed by creating places of belonging that cater to their needs. For far too long, older congregation members have been taken for granted, even if in a well-meaning way. Several pastors and rabbis were surveyed for background research on this book and while all stated what a blessing it is to have the foundational leaders among them and reap the benefits of their knowledge and wisdom, very few were able to point to specific programs or accommodations that have been made for their older members. And the reason behind that is no one's fault; our demographics are completely different from what they were a generation ago, or at any point in history for that matter. There is no manual that exists to teach the world how to adapt to this new environment.

That is the reason for this book. By gaining a deeper understanding of the complex layers of challenges that often accompany older adulthood and then looking at the tools that are currently available to mitigate those challenges, faith communities can now begin to write their own manuals. Places of worship can move away from the expectation that all older adults will automatically stay and serve the congregation until they die; they can move away from the notion that "this is what has always worked for us in the past, so it should work for us now too".

4 Ways to Retain Older Adults

1. Physical accessibility- modifications and transportation that make things safer and easier.
2. Addressing social isolation- creating opportunities outside of worship for engagement.
3. Meaningful engagement- creating opportunities to serve others using one's gifts and talents.
4. Dispelling stereotypes- having open and honest conversations that eradicate ageism and connect multiple generations.

RetirementReformation.org. "Embracing the Silver and Gold: Recognizing the Unique Needs of Our Older Adults". May 16.

The payoff for adapting to meet the needs of older members is huge, and it means everything for the future health and growth of the faith community. In a blog post on RetirementReformation.org[5], several successes were highlighted:

5. See RetirementReformation.org, "Embracing the Silver and Gold"

Part 3: Challenge as Opportunity

1. A church in Austin, Texas "rallied together to adapt their historic building, preserving its traditional charm while incorporating modern, accessible features. Ramps replaced steps, elevators were installed, and comfortable seating was arranged, ensuring that everyone could enjoy the service without physical discomfort. But this church didn't stop at architectural modifications. They looked beyond the church walls and extended their inclusivity to the journey to church as well. Volunteers were rallied, schedules were coordinated, and soon, a transportation system was in place. Older adults who previously found the journey arduous were now being picked up from their homes and brought to church."

2. A congregation near Chicago "established various groups, each catering to the interests and needs of their older adults. These groups were not merely formed but were nurtured with care and commitment. Social outings were planned, allowing the older adults to step out of their daily routines and experience new sights and sounds. Bible studies were organized, offering a platform for spiritual growth and fellowship. Perhaps most surprisingly, tech lessons were introduced. Older adults were taught how to use technology to connect with their loved ones and the world around them."

3. A church in Denver "recognized the untapped potential within their older adults and decided to create avenues for meaningful engagement. They started by simply asking their older adults about their interests, skills, and how they'd like to contribute to the church community. The response was overwhelming."

4. And a congregation in Augusta, Maine "made a conscious effort to challenge these assumptions, starting with open conversations about ageism within their community. They invited their older adults to share their experiences, aspirations, and frustrations, which were eye-opening for many of the younger members.

These conversations led to a change in the church's approach. Older adults were no longer seen through the narrow lens of age-related stereotypes but were appreciated for their individual strengths and capabilities. This shift in perception led to a more inclusive, empowering environment for all members of the congregation."

This recent Facebook post sums up everything perfectly: "Germantown United Methodist Church welcomed Joanna D. into membership

Member Retention

on Sunday, June 30 at our 8:30 traditional worship service. She joined by transfer of her membership from First Presbyterian Church, Jackson, TN. Her Welcome Friend is Dorothy R. When asked what about Germantown UMC made her want to become a part of our church community, she replied, "When I looked at the GUMC website and saw how many Sunday school classes and activities GUMC had for seniors, I thought, these people care about all ages of their congregation. I have been impressed with all the people at GUMC that I have been in contact with. Everyone is so welcoming, and they make me feel like I finally found a home. I look forward to this next chapter in my life with the church and I hope I will be a good member like all the ones that have been so nice to me!"[6]

> Reframing Aging. "As church leaders we are called to help change attitudes in our congregations about aging. We need to first recognize the negative attitudes we may have about our own aging and that of older adults in general. We can teach our congregation by example and serve as advocates on behalf of aging and older adults. When we reframe aging—ours and others—we are challenging the cultural myths of growing older. By reframing aging, we see older adulthood not as an age of liability but as an age of opportunity".
> Rev. Dr. Richard H. Gentzler Jr., 2020. "Reframing Aging in Churches", *ENCORE Ministry Matters*. December 2020 issue. EncoreMinistry.org

---

6. See Germantown United Methodist Church, Facebook post

Conclusion

THE WORLD AND FAITH as we know it is changing. Through the miracles of science, technology, medicine, and knowledge, people are living longer than they ever have before. For the first time in history, there will be more people over the age of 65 than people under age 18 and with that enormous shift in society comes a lot of issues that have not been seen previously on so large a scale.

Where communities of faith once stood as beacons of hope, a moral compass, and a place of fellowship with other believers, now has become to many older adults a place that is inaccessible, unsupportive, and irrelevant. The secret to helping faith communities and older adults get back to that place of hope is meeting older adults where they are and addressing their unique needs.

If the building is now too inaccessible and increases an older member's risk of falling, the solution is to do safety audits and make changes that will produce a safer and more welcoming environment. If older members that have dementia no longer feel included or welcomed at their church or synagogue, then the solution is making inclusive programs available, educating the congregation on better ways to communicate, and making the environment safer. If older members can no longer participate in worship due to vision and hearing loss, the solution is to redesign written and oral communications. If older members are suffering from social isolation, the solution is to have programming that accommodates their abilities and mobilizes to include them where they are. If older adults can no longer attend services due to caring for a loved one, the solution is to have programs that offer respite and support. If older members are being victimized at the hands of others, the solution is to be a safe space where they can receive help. If an older adult is struggling with family issues and estrangement, the solution is helping families learn to communicate better so they can heal. If an older member is struggling to have enough food to eat or struggling to have a place to live, or struggling with transportation, the solution is to have policies and programs in place to meet those needs.

However, focusing on meeting the needs of older members is only one part of the equation; the health and future growth of the faith community depends heavily upon the bonds of its members. Intergenerational programs and health-focused ministries connect members of all ages and stages of life so that they can operate as one unit, one body of believers.

But before any changes take place, it is necessary to get people talking and acknowledging the things that need to be changed. Older members need to feel heard and seen and have their thoughts, opinions, and ideas taken into consideration. The way to get people talking is through surveys and focus groups. Then once people start talking and issues are presented, it becomes a process to effect intentional change that has the flexibility to evolve over time as the congregation's needs change.

And finally, the secret to helping faith communities and older adults get back to that place of hope is understanding what draws older members away from the community and remembering the why- why does the place of worship exist and why did the members form a congregation to begin with? Getting to the heart of member retention involves not taking the foundations on which the community was built for granted, and making those foundational members feel loved and appreciated by acknowledging and understanding their challenges as well as actively working together to solve problems.

Becoming an Age-Friendly Community of Faith is a journey that takes time and buy-in from the congregation. It is a constant process of learning what challenges exist, what possible solutions there might be, receiving feedback, implementing changes, re-evaluating changes, and adapting to new challenges, while simultaneously being focused on the overall mission to love God and love others.

Conclusion

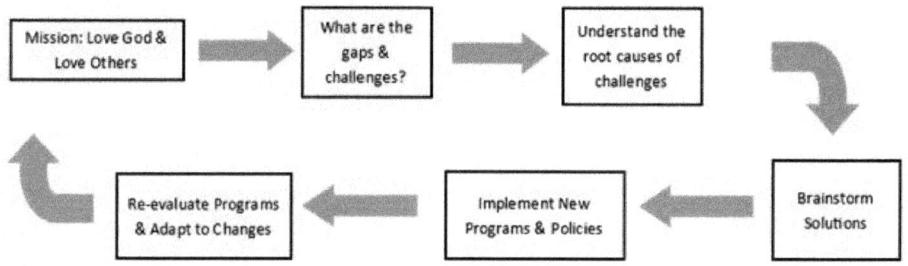

The end result of this process is a healthy, mission-focused faith community that becomes a lifelong home to its members and a shining light of love and service in the neighborhood, where members can deepen their faith because they are in a place of acceptance and belonging.

It is hoped that the tools and resources in this book can guide your congregation to a deeper level of understanding and help transform your community into one that is friendly to all ages and abilities.

Glossary of Terms

Activities of Daily Living (ADLs)- The ability or inability to bathe, dress, feed, toilet, and transfer oneself.

Adult Daycare- A place where a person with dementia can go during the day for socialization, activities, and a meal so that their caregiver can go to work or attend to other household needs.

Adult Protective Services- An agency in each state that receives complaints and investigates cases of abuse and neglect of vulnerable adults.

Advanced Directive- A document that allows a person to name a healthcare proxy, which terminal health conditions are acceptable or unacceptable, and which treatments for those conditions are acceptable or unacceptable. A plain language version is available through The Five Wishes.

Affordable Housing (aka Subsidized Housing)- Independent Living residences that are partially funded by the Department of Housing and Urban Development. A person pays no more than 30% of his or her income for rent.

Age-Friendly Public Health Systems- Treating older adults through the lens of The 4 M's- Mobility, Medication, Mentation, and What Matters. Mobility includes one's ability to walk, operate an assistive device, transfer to/from sitting and standing, etc. Medication includes examining the amount and types of medication a person takes to see what can be reduced or eliminated. Mentation includes one's emotional health and cognition. What Matters includes finding out what is most important to a person, what motivates them to be compliant with their care, and honoring their wishes.

Glossary of Terms

Assisted Living- A residential setting that provides older adults with assistance in Activities of Daily Living, as well as provides meals, medication management, transportation, and activities.

Continuing Care Retirement Community- A residential setting that includes various levels of care on one campus, from independent living to assisted living to memory care and skilled nursing care.

Home Healthcare- A short-term outpatient program that consists of visits from nurses and therapists at one's home following a hospital stay. It must be ordered by a doctor and is covered by health insurance.

Hospice- An outpatient program for those who are terminally ill that provides in-home visits from nurses, social workers, and chaplains to provide comfort measures at the end of life. It must be ordered by a doctor and is covered by health insurance.

Independent Living- A residential setting wherein an older adult must be capable of caring for their own needs and affairs, although some outside help (such a housekeeper) is generally acceptable.

Instrumental Activities of Daily Living (IADLs)- The ability or inability to complete tasks such as shopping, housekeeping, managing finances, managing medications, and communication.

Long-Term Care Insurance- An insurance policy that can pay a portion of costs associated with non-medical home care, assisted living, memory care, and skilled nursing care.

Long-Term Care Ombudsman- A person who receives complaints about care in residential facilities and investigates allegations of resident abuse and neglect.

Low-Income Subsidy- A benefit that can help reduce the cost of prescription drugs for individuals who qualify.

Medicaid- Subsidies for healthcare administered by each state that may include assistance with monthly Medicare premiums, costs not covered by Medicare Parts A and B, prescription drugs, and long-term care in a skilled nursing facility.

Medicare Part A- Coverage for inpatient hospital stays, rehab, skilled nursing, home healthcare, and hospice care.

Glossary of Terms

Medicare Part B- Coverage for doctors appointments, diagnostics, outpatient procedures, physical/occupational/speech therapy, medical equipment, emergency ambulance, and preventative medicine.

Medicare Part C- Coverage for vision, dental, and hearing. Only available in Medicare Advantage Plans.

Medicare Part D- Coverage for prescription drugs.

Medicare Advantage Plans- Plans administered through private insurance companies that bundle Medicare Parts A & B, Part C, and Part D benefits together, along with additional benefits such as gym memberships, medical transportation, etc. Most plans do not have an additional monthly premium aside from the standard Medicare Part B monthly premium.

Medicare Savings Plans- A form of Medicaid that can help reduce healthcare costs.

Medicare Supplement Plans- Plans administered through private insurance companies that cover the costs of healthcare not covered by Medicare Parts A and B. Plans do not include dental, vision, hearing, or drug benefits.

Memory Care- A secure residential setting that provides older adults with dementia assistance with Activities of Daily Living, as well as meals, medication management, transportation, and activities. Memory Care may be a stand-alone facility or part of an assisted living.

Non-Medical Homecare- A service provided by private companies that offers assistance with Activities of Daily Living, meal preparation, light housekeeping, transportation, medication reminders, and companionship.

Palliative Care- A long-term outpatient program that provides visits in the home from nurses, therapists, social workers, and chaplains for those who have complex chronic conditions. It must be ordered by a doctor and is covered by health insurance.

Powers of Attorney- Legal documents that name a healthcare proxy and a fiduciary in the event that a person is unable to make decisions for themselves.

Glossary of Terms

Respite- A short-term stay in an assisted living or skilled nursing facility that can allow a caregiver to travel, recover from surgery, etc. It is not covered by insurance unless a person is under hospice care.

Skilled Nursing Care- A residential setting that provides care for all Activities of Daily Living, meals, housekeeping, medication management, and activities, as well as skilled care tasks such as wound and ostomy care, tracheostomy and ventilator care, dialysis, etc. Skilled nursing facilities may also provide short-term rehab and convalescence following a hospital stay.

SNAP (Supplemental Nutrition Assistance Program)- A monthly benefit that an eligible person can use towards groceries.

Social Security- A monthly benefit based on how many quarters a person worked and how much they paid into Social Security taxes.

Supplemental Security Income (SSI)- An additional monthly benefit for those who are in the lowest income categories.

Trust- A legal document that can protect a person's estate and assets from Medicaid Estate Recovery and probate.

VA Aid & Attendance- A benefit program for eligible veterans and their spouses that can provide a monthly dollar amount to use towards non-medical homecare, assisted living, memory care, and skilled nursing care.

Will- A legal document that describes a person's estate and how they would like their assets to be distributed upon death.

Resources

BOOKS

1. A Time to Prepare Edited by Richard F. Address and the Commission on Jewish Family Concerns
2. Accessible Gospel, Inclusive Worship by Barbara J. Newman and Betty Grit. Available on Amazon.com
3. Aging and Ministry in the 21st Century: An Inquiry Approach by Richard H. Gentzler, Jr. Available on Amazon.com
4. An Age of Opportunity: Intentional Ministry by, with, and for Older Adults by Richard H. Gentzler. Available on Amazon.com
5. And God Created Hope: Finding Your Way Through Grief with Lessons from Early Biblical Stories by Rabbi Mel Glazer. Available on Amazon.com
6. Asserting Yourself-Updated Edition: A Practical Guide For Positive Change by Sharon Anthony Bower and Gordon H. Bower
7. Caring Assertiveness by Kenneth Haugk, Joel Bretscher, and Robert Musser. Available at CaringAssertiveness.org
8. Dementia-Friendly Worship by L. Everman, D. Wendorf, K. Berry, R. Dill, S. Glazer, R. Morgan, and W. Randolph. Available on Amazon.com
9. Don't Sing Songs to a Heavy Heart: How to Relate to Those Who Are Suffering by Kenneth Haugk. Available on StephenMinistries.org

Resources

10. Don't Write My Obituary Just Yet: Inspiring Faith Stories for Older Adults by Missy Buchanan. Available on UpperRoom.org
11. Engage All Generations: A Strategic Toolkit for Creating Intergenerational Faith Communities by Cory Seibel. Available on Amazon.com
12. Faith and Mental Health: Religious Resources for Healing by Dr. Harold Koenig. Available on Amazon.com
13. Feeling Your Way Through Grief by Missy Buchanan. Available on Amazon.com
14. InterGenerate: Transforming Churches through Intergenerational Ministry by Holly Catterton Allen and Jason Brian Santos. Available on Amazon.com
15. Intergenerational Christian Formation: Bringing the Whole Church Together in Ministry, Community, and Worship by Holly Catterton Allen, Christine Lawton, and Cory L. Seibel. Available on Amazon.com
16. Journeying Through Grief- 4 part series by Kenneth Haugk. Available on StephenMinistries.org
17. Joy Boosters: 120 Ways to Encourage Older Adults by Missy Buchanan. Available on UpperRoom.org
18. Living with Purpose in a Worn-Out Body: Spiritual Encouragement for Older Adults by Missy Buchanan. Available on UpperRoom.org
19. Mended: Restoring the Hearts of Mothers and Daughters by Blythe Daniel and Dr. Helen McIntosh. Available at ChristianBook.com
20. Ministry with the Forgotten: Dementia through a Spiritual Lens by Kenneth Carder. Available on Amazon.com
21. No Act of Love is Ever Wasted: The Spirituality of Caring for Persons with Dementia by Jane Marie Thibault and Richard L. Morgan. Available on Amazon.com
22. Pastoral Care of Older Adults by Harold G. Koenig and Andrew J. Weaver. Available on Amazon.com
23. Pilgrimage into the Last Third of Life: 7 Gateways to Spiritual Growth by Jane Marie Thibault. Available on Amazon.com
24. Purpose and Power in Retirement: New Opportunities for Meaning and Significance by Dr. Harold Koenig. Available on Amazon.com

Resources

25. Reclaiming Joy Together: Building a Volunteer Community of Real Hope for Those with Dementia by Daphne Johnston and Dr. Lawson Bryan. Available on Amazon.com

26. Safe Sanctuaries: The Church Responds to Abuse, Neglect, and Exploitation by Joy Thornton Melton. Available at Cokesbury.com

27. Seasons of Caring: Meditations for Alzheimer's and Dementia Caregivers by Clergy Against Alzheimer's Network. Available on Amazon.com

28. Seekers of Meaning: Baby Boomers, Judaism, and the Pursuit of Healthy Aging by Rabbi Richard Address. Available on Amazon.com

29. Senior Cohousing: A Community Approach to Independent Living by Charles Durrett. Available on Amazon.com

30. Spiritual Care for People Living with Dementia Using Multisensory Interventions by Richard Behers. Available on Amazon.com

31. Talking with God In Old Age: Meditations and Psalms by Missy Buchanan. Available on UpperRoom.org

32. The Gift of Empathy by Joel Bretscher and Kenneth Haugk. Available on StephenMinistries.org

33. The Graying of the Church: A Leader's Guide for Older-Adult Ministry in the United Methodist Church by Richard H. Gentzler, Jr. Available on Amazon.com

34. The Health Cabinet: How to Start a Wellness Committee in Your Church by Jill Westberg-McNamara. Available on Amazon.com

35. The Lafiya Guide: A Congregational Handbook for Whole-Person Health Ministry by Assoc. of Brethren Caregivers Staff. Available on Amazon.com

36. Unlikely Teachers: Finding the Hidden Gifts in Daily Conflict by Judy Ringer. Available on Amazon.com

37. Voices of Aging: Adult Children and Aging Parents Talk with God by Missy Buchanan. Available on UpperRoom.org

38. Walking With Grace: Tools For Implementing And Launching A Congregational Respite Program by Robin Dill. Available on Amazon.com

39. You and Your Aging Parent: A Family Guide to Emotional, Social, Health, and Financial Problems by Barbara Silverstone and Helen

RESOURCES

Kandel Hyman with commentary by Bob Morris. Available on Amazon.com

WEBSITES

1. Administration for Community Living. Connection to resources. Found at ACL.gov > What Do You Need Help With?

2. Advocate Faith Community Nurse Program. Found at AdvocateHealth.com

3. Alter Dementia training for faith communities. Found at AlterDementia.com

4. Alzheimer's Association. Found at Alz.org

5. Caregiving programs directory. Found at BPC.Caregiver.org

6. Christian Community Health Fellowship. Found at CCHF.org

7. Church Health Assessment Tool. Found at HealthyChurch.net

8. Co-Housing Association of the United States. Found at CoHousing.org

9. Congregational Resource Guide. Curated wellness ministry resources. Found at TheCRG.org > Collections > Wellness Ministry

10. Connect2Affect. Social Isolation Assessment Tool. Found at Connect2Affect.org

11. Eldercare Locator Directory. Found at USAging.org > Find Local Aging Services

12. Dementia Friends USA. Found at DementiaFriendsUSA.org

13. Dementia-Friendly Faith Community Guide. Found at DFAmerica.org

14. Diverse Elders Coalition. Resources and advocacy for LGBTQIA+ elders. Found at DiverseElders.org

15. Faith Community Engagement Blueprint. Found at TheCTAC.org > Blog/Resources > Toolkits

16. Family Caregiver Alliance. Articles and resource directory for caregivers. Found at Caregiver.org

Resources

17. Federal Deposit Insurance Corporation. "Money Smart for Older Adults" Program. Found at FDIC.gov > Resources > Consumer Resource Center > Money Smart

18. Federal Trade Commission. Free print publications on a variety of topics related to scams and fraud. Found at FTC.gov > Bulk Publications (bottom of page)

19. Five Wishes End-of-Life Planning Tool. Found at FiveWishes.org

20. GenOnMinistries.org. Toolkits and resources for building intergenerational faith communities.

21. GoGoGrandparent.com. Ride share platform for older adults

22. GriefShare.org. Grief Support Group program.

23. Home and Driving Safety Guidebooks. Found at TheHartford.com > Resources > Mature Market Excellence

24. Interfaith Health Program. Faith-based and public health partnerships. Found at IHPEmory.org > Programs

25. Intergenerational Church Toolkit. Found at CRCNA.org/FaithFormation/Toolkits

26. JewishSacredAging.com. Blog, podcast, books and resources on faith and aging.

27. Johnson Institute for Spiritual Gerontology and Lifelong Adult Faith Formation. Found at SeniorAdultMinistry.com

28. KavodvNichum.org. Jewish death and grief resources.

29. Lichtenberg Older Adult Nest Egg. Financial vulnerability assessment tool and older adult resources. Found at OlderAdultNestEgg.com

30. LifelongFaith.com. Publications and resources for ministry across lifespans.

31. LittleFreePantry.org. Directory and instructions on how to start your own.

32. Living Abundantly Ministries. Evidence-based program that combines physical and spiritual wellbeing. Found at LivingAbundantlyMinistries.org

33. Memory Café Directory. Found at DFAmerica.org > Memory Café Alliance

RESOURCES

34. Mom's Meals food delivery service. Found at MomsMeals.org
35. National Alliance on Caregiving. Found at Caregiving.org
36. National Center on Elder Abuse. Found at NCEA.ACL.gov
37. National Council on Aging. Articles on healthy aging and caregiving. Found at NCOA.org
38. National Long-Term Care Ombudsman Resource Center. Found at NORC.ACL.gov
39. NationalGleaningProject.org. Directory and resources for starting your own gleaning ministry.
40. National Institute on Aging. Free print publications on a variety of topics related to aging. Found at NIA.NIH.gov > Print Publications
41. Network of Jewish Human Service Agencies. National directory of Jewish Family Services and other partners. Found at NetworkJHSA.org
42. Nutrition & Aging Resource Center. Found at ACL.gov/Senior-Nutrition > Browse Resources
43. Powerful Tools for Caregivers training classes. Found at PowerfulToolsForCaregivers.org
44. Prepare For Your Care End-of-Life Planning. Found at PrepareForYourCare.org
45. ReframingAging.org. Resources and initiative to reframe ageist stereotypes.
46. Respite Ministry Roadmap. Found at RespiteForAll.org
47. SageUSA.org. Resources and advocacy for LGBTQIA+ elders
48. Samara Care Counseling. Congregational Care and Consulting. Found at SamaraCareCounsling.org
49. Sample Community Needs Assessment. Found at OPRP.DOR.org > Resources > Community Needs Assessment
50. Spiritual Eldercare video series. Found at YouTube.com > Spiritual Eldercare
51. StephenMinistries.org
52. Supporting Caregivers in Jewish Congregations. Found at TheCTAC.org > Blog/Resources > Toolkits

Resources

53. Talking Elder Abuse Toolkit. A toolkit designed to enhance awareness and education of elder abuse. Found at FrameworksInstitute.org/toolkit/talking-elder-abuse

54. The Center for Faith and Community Health Transformation. Models, toolkits, and resources for implementing a health ministry. Found at FaithHealthTransformation.org

55. Thinking Ahead Roadmap financial planning tool. Found at ThinkingAheadRoadmap.org

56. United Church of Christ Wellness Ministries Toolkit. Found at UCC.org > How We Serve > Love of Church > Education for Faithful Action Ministries

57. United Methodist Church Older Adult Ministries. Found at EncoreMinistry.org

58. UsAgainstAlzheimers.org > Networks > Faith > Creating Dementia Friendly Faith Communities

59. Village to Village Network. Found at VTVNetwork.org

60. Well Connected. Programs for older adults via phone or Zoom. Found at FrontPorch.net > Connect > Well Connected

61. Westburg Institute for Faith Community Nursing. Originally known as the International Parish Nurse Resource Center. Found at WestburgInstitute.org

Bibliography

Alzheimer's Association. 2024. "2024 Alzheimer's Disease Facts and Figures." Alzheimer's Association. https://www.alz.org/media/Documents/alzheimers-facts-and-figures.pdf.
American Bar Association. 2022. Adult Protective Services Reporting Laws. https://www.americanbar.org/content/dam/aba/administrative/law_aging/2020-elder-abuse-reporting-chart.pdf.
American Optometric Association. n.d. "Adult Vision: 41 to 60 Years of Age." www.aoa.org. https://www.aoa.org/healthy-eyes/eye-health-for-life/adult-vision-41-to-60-years-of-age.
Arkansas Baptists State Convention. "Conducting a Church Assessment." https://www.absc.org/files/uploads/ConductingaChurchAssessment.pdf.
"Assertiveness." *AtHealth.com*, October 23, 2013. https://athealth.com/topics/assertiveness-3/.
Association of Brethren Caregivers. *Agents of Healing Workshop Materials: The Lafiya Guide: A Congregational Handbook for Whole-Person Health Ministry*. 1993. https://www.faithhealthtransformation.org/wp-content/uploads/2015/12/Health-Wellness-Ministry-Why-Should-the-Church-Get-Involved.pdf.
Bulos, Gemma. 2023. "Caring for Aging Parents Doesn't Have to Be This Hard." Los Angeles Times, November 5, 2023. https://www.latimes.com/opinion/story/2023-11-05/old-elderly-aging-senior-parents-families-caregiver-immigrant-home-healthcare.
Bridging the Gap. "Inclusive and Accessible Communication Guidelines." https://bridgingthegap-project.eu/wp-content/uploads/BtG_Inclusive-and-accessible-Communication-Guidelines.pdf.
"Caregiving in the U.S. 2020 Age 50+." 2020, May. https://doi.org/10.26419/ppi.00103.022.
The Center for Faith and Community Health Transformation. "Faith-Based Approaches for Promoting Health." https://www.faithhealthtransformation.org/resources-and-toolkits/developing-a-health-ministry/health-ministries-in-action/.
Centers for Disease Control and Prevention. 2021. "Facts about Falls." www.cdc.gov, August 6, 2021. https://www.cdc.gov/falls/facts.html.
Centers for Disease Control and Prevention. 2021. "Loneliness and Social Isolation Linked to Serious Health Conditions." Alzheimer's Disease and Healthy Aging, 2021. https://www.cdc.gov/aging/publications/features/lonely-older-adults.html.

Bibliography

Centers for Disease Control and Prevention. 2024. "About Abuse of Older Persons." Abuse of Older Persons, August 22, 2024. https://www.cdc.gov/elder-abuse/about/index.html#cdc_behavioral_basics_quick-quick-facts-and-stats

Christian Reformed Church. "Intergenerational Church Toolkit." https://www.crcna.org/FaithFormation/toolkits/intergenerational-church-toolkit.

Christian Reformed Church. "25 Ideas for Intergenerational Service." 2016. https://www.crcna.org/sites/default/files/25_ideas_for_intergenerational_service.pdf.

Church Tech Today. "Assisted Listening Systems for Church Sound." July 7, 2017. https://churchtechtoday.com/assisted-listening-systems-church-sound/.

Cleveland Clinic. 2023. "What Is Grief?" Cleveland Clinic, February 22, 2023. https://my.clevelandclinic.org/health/diseases/24787-grief.

"Cost of Long Term Care by State | Cost of Care Report." n.d. www.genworth.com. https://www.genworth.com/aging-and-you/finances/cost-of-care.

Costley, A. "Aging in A Food Desert: Differences in Food Access Among Older and Younger Adults." *Innov Aging* 2, no. suppl 1 (November 11, 2018): 328. https://doi.org/10.1093/geroni/igy023.1202. PMCID: PMC6227553.

Daniel, Blythe. "Family Estrangement: 6 Ways to Reconcile with Adult Children." *Focus on the Family*, September 30, 2024. https://www.focusonthefamily.com/parenting/family-estrangement-6-ways-to-reconcile-with-adult-children/.

Durrett, Charles. "Senior Cohousing: A Community Approach to Independent Living." *American Society on Aging*, June 21, 2023. https://generations.asaging.org/cohousing-way-solo-agers-gain-community.

Earls, Aaron. "5 Current Church Attendance Trends You Need to Know." *Lifeway Research*, February 2, 2022. https://research.lifeway.com/2022/02/02/5-current-church-attendance-trends-you-need-to-know/.

Eisenberg, Richard. "New Solutions to Older Adults' Housing Challenges." Next Avenue, November 21, 2023. https://www.nextavenue.org/new-solutions-housing-challenges/.

Family Caregiver Alliance. 2016. "Caregiver Statistics: Demographics." Family Caregiver Alliance, 2016. https://www.caregiver.org/resource/caregiver-statistics-demographics/.

Federal Bureau of Investigation. 2019. "Elder Fraud, in Focus | Federal Bureau of Investigation." Federal Bureau of Investigation, 2019. https://www.fbi.gov/news/stories/elder-fraud-in-focus.

Federal Bureau of Investigation. n.d. "How We Can Help You. Scams and Safety. Elder Fraud." www.fbi.gov. https://www.fbi.gov/how-we-can-help-you/scams-and-safety/common-scams-and-crimes/elder-fraud.

Feeding America. 2025. "Understanding Hunger and Food Insecurity." Feedingamerica.org, Feeding America, 2025. https://www.feedingamerica.org/hunger-in-america/food-insecurity.

Fivecoat-Campbell, Kerri. "Trapped in the Affordable Housing Gap." *Next Avenue*, March 16, 2023. https://www.nextavenue.org/trapped-in-the-affordable-housing-gap/.

Flowers, Lynda, Ari Houser, et al. 2017. "Insight on the Issues Medicare Spends More on Socially Isolated Older Adults." https://www.aarp.org/content/dam/aarp/ppi/2017/10/medicare-spends-more-on-socially-isolated-older-adults.pdf.

Freedman, Amy, and Jennifer Nicolle. 2020. "Social Isolation and Loneliness: The New Geriatric Giants: Approach for Primary Care." *Canadian Family Physician Medecin de Famille Canadien* 66 (3): 176–82. https://pubmed.ncbi.nlm.nih.gov/32165464/.

Bibliography

Gentzler, Richard H. Jr. "S.E.N.I.O.R.S. Ministry." *Circuit Rider*, February 1, 2009. https://www.ministrymatters.com/all/entry/112/seniors-ministry.

Gerlach, Lauren B., Erica S. Solway, and Preeti N. Malani. 2024. "Social Isolation and Loneliness in Older Adults." JAMA 331 (23): 2058. https://doi.org/10.1001/jama.2024.3456.

Germantown United Methodist Church. "Facebook Post." July 7, 2024.

Graham, Judith. n.d. "Do We Just Not Care about Old People?" USA TODAY. https://www.usatoday.com/story/news/health/2024/03/01/old-people-ageism-health-covid/72597190007/.

Graves, Ginny. n.d. "10 Signs That You Could Have Hearing Loss." AARP. https://www.aarp.org/health/conditions-treatments/info-2021/hearing-loss-signs.html.

"Grown Children Who Ignore Their Parents: Seniors and Family Estrangement." *GreatSeniorLiving.com*, February 24, 2022. https://www.greatseniorliving.com/articles/grown-children-who-ignore-parents.

HEAR Center. 2022. "How Does Your Hearing Change as You Age?" Hear Center, April 25, 2022. https://www.hearcenter.org/how-does-your-hearing-change-as-you-age/.

Herman, Laura. "7 Forms of Elder Abuse & How to Recognize the Abuse of Seniors." *SafeSeniorCare.com*, March 6, 2023. https://saferseniorcare.com/types-of-elder-abuse/.

"How to Start a Food Pantry at Your Church: A Step-by-Step Plan." *SuperFoodHelp.com*, March 8, 2024. https://www.superfoodhelp.com/knowledge/how-to-start-a-food-pantry-at-your-church.

Johns Hopkins Medicine. 2020. "Types of Hearing Loss." Johns Hopkins Medicine, 2020. https://www.hopkinsmedicine.org/health/conditions-and-diseases/hearing-loss/types-of-hearing-loss.

Jones, Jeffery M. "Church Attendance Has Declined in Most U.S. Religious Groups." *Gallup*, March 25, 2024. https://news.gallup.com/poll/642548/church-attendance-declined-religious-groups.aspx.

Kaiser Family Foundation. 2024. "Status of State Medicaid Expansion Decisions: Interactive Map." Kaiser Family Foundation, November 12, 2024. https://www.kff.org/affordable-care-act/issue-brief/status-of-state-medicaid-expansion-decisions-interactive-map/.

Kehrwald, Leif, and John Roberto. "Insights from Research & Theory: Practices for Forming Faith Intergenerationally." *LifelongFaith.com*, 2023. https://www.lifelongfaith.com/uploads/5/1/6/4/5164069/practices_for_forming_faith_-_intergenerational__lfa_.pdf.

Kibbey, Sue Nilson. "A Spiritually Inviting Food Pantry." *ChurchLeadership.com*, January 11, 2017. https://www.churchleadership.com/leading-ideas/spiritually-inviting-food-pantry/.

Lin, Frank R. MD, PhD. 2021. "Hearing Loss and the Dementia Connection | Johns Hopkins Bloomberg School of Public Health." Publichealth.jhu.edu, November 12, 2021. https://publichealth.jhu.edu/2021/hearing-loss-and-the-dementia-connection.

Linthicum, Dorothy. "Faith Formation after 70: Ministry with Older Adults." *Building Faith*, May 16, 2016. https://buildfaith.org/faith-formation-older-adults/.

MacInnis, Adam. "The Church Is Losing Its Gray Heads." *Lifeway Research*, March 2022. https://www.christianitytoday.com/2022/02/gray-gen-x-boomers-older-churchgoers-leaving-church/.

Bibliography

Mather, Mark, and Paola Scommegna. 2024. "Fact Sheet: Aging in the United States." Population Reference Bureau, January 9, 2024. https://www.prb.org/resources/fact-sheet-aging-in-the-united-states/.

Matteson, Peggy S. "Health Ministry: Providing for Health and Wholeness Within a Congregation." *Common Lot*, Fall 2003, no. 99: 4–6.

"Mayo Clinic." n.d. "Dementia—Symptoms and Causes." https://www.mayoclinic.org/diseases-conditions/dementia.

"Mid-South Congregational Health Needs Assessment, Planning, and Follow-up Tools and Protocols." Developed through a partnership between: Methodist Le Bonheur Healthcare, Congregational Health Network; Church Health, Faith Community Engagement; National Faith-Based Mobilization Network; YOUR Center; University of Memphis School of Public Health; Johns Hopkins Bloomberg School of Public Health (PI: Dr. Brook Harmon, bharmon1@memphis.edu or harmonbe1@appstate.edu; Project Contact: Dr. Jonathan Lewis, jonathan.lewis@mlh.org). https://nutrition.appstate.edu/sites/default/files/BrookHarmon/packet_mschs_plan_follow-up_8.4.20.pdf.

Mikhail, Alexa. 2023. "1 in 5 Older Adults Don't Have Someone They Can Depend on in Time of Need. It's Driving up ER Visits and Food Insecurity." Fortune Well, Fortune, November 7, 2023. https://fortune.com/well/2023/11/07/older-adults-loneliness-isolation-emergency-room-visits.

Mohamed, Maiss, Molly O'Malley Watts. 2023. "Pandemic-Era Changes to Medicaid Home- and Community-Based Services (HCBS): A Closer Look at Family Caregiver Policies." KFF. https://www.kff.org/medicaid/issue-brief/pandemic-era-changes-to-medicaid-home-and-community-based-services-hcbs-a-closer-look-at-family-caregiver-policies/.

Moravian.org. "Church Needs Assessment Template." https://www.moravian.org/bcm/wp-content/uploads/sites/2/2020/05/Congregational-Needs-Assessment-Template.pdf.

National Alliance on Caregiving. 2020. "Caregiving in the U.S. 2020 Report." Infographic. https://www.caregiving.org/wp-content/uploads/2020/05/AARP-835-AARP-Caregiving-in-the-US-Infographics-vFINAL-1.pdf.

National Alliance to End Homelessness. "Who Experiences Homelessness: Older Adults." December 2023. https://endhomelessness.org/homelessness-in-america/who-experiences-homelessness/older-adults/.

National Center on Elder Abuse. 2023. "NCEA | Elder Abuse." Ncea.acl.gov, December 26, 2023. https://ncea.acl.gov/elder-abuse#gsc.tab=0.

National Center on Elder Abuse. n.d. "NCEA | Risk Factors & Protective Factors." Ncea.acl.gov. https://ncea.acl.gov/riskfactorsandprotectivefactors#gsc.tab=0.

National Council on Aging. 2022. "Get the Facts on Food Insecurity and Older Adults." www.ncoa.org, April 15, 2022. https://www.ncoa.org/article/what-is-food-insecurity-get-the-facts.

National Council on Aging. "Seniors & SNAP: 5 Myths Busted." April 4, 2022. https://www.ncoa.org/article/seniors-snap-5-myths-busted.

National Institute on Aging. 2020. "Social Isolation, Loneliness in Older People Pose Health Risks." National Institute on Aging, April 23, 2020. https://www.nia.nih.gov/news/social-isolation-loneliness-older-people-pose-health-risks.

Prange-Morgan, Chris. "What Is 'Spoon Theory'? And Why Is It Important?" *PsychologyToday.com*, April 17, 2024. https://www.psychologytoday.com/us/blog/full-catastrophe-parenting/202403/what-is-spoon-theory-and-why-is-it-important.

Bibliography

"Recognizing Self-Neglect." 2016. Self-Neglect, November 28, 2016. https://selfneglect.org/self-neglect-facts/self-neglect-basics/recognizing-self-neglect/.

RetirementReformation.org. "Embracing the Silver and Gold: Recognizing the Unique Needs of Our Older Adults." May 16. https://retirementreformation.org/blog/embracing-the-silver-and-gold-recognizing-the-unique-needs-of-our-older-adults.

Ringer, Judy. "The Aikido of Communication." CompleteWellbeing.com, May 1, 2017. https://completewellbeing.com/article/the-aikido-of-communication/.

Roach, David. "Church Attendance Dropped Among Young People, Singles, Liberals." Christianity Today, January 9, 2023. https://www.christianitytoday.com/2023/01/pandemic-church-attendance-drop-aei-survey-young-people-eva/.

Roberto, John. Lifelong Faith Formation for All Ages and Generations, January 18, 2022, 56–57.

Roman Catholic Archdiocese of Atlanta. "Parish Needs Assessment." https://archatl.com/pastoral-plan/evolution-of-our-parishes/parish-need-assessment/.

Roman Catholic Diocese of Rochester. Office of Pastoral Resources and Planning. "Conducting a Community Needs Assessment." https://oprp.dor.org/wp-content/uploads/2016/10/Community-Needs-Assessment-With-Survey.pdf.

Satterfield, Ken. "Senior Adult Ministries Key to Church's Future." Word & Way, September 7, 2016. https://wordandway.org/2016/09/07/senior-adult-ministries-key-to-church-s-future/.

"Senior Vision: Over 60 Years of Age." 2024. Aoa.org, 2024. https://www.aoa.org/healthy-eyes/eye-health-for-life/senior-vision.

Silverstone, Barbara, and Helen Kandel Hyman. 2008. You and Your Aging Parent. Oxford University Press.

The R.L. Mace Universal Design Institute. "Universal Design Principles." https://www.udinstitute.org/principles.

"The State of Senior Hunger | Feeding America." n.d. www.feedingamerica.org. https://www.feedingamerica.org/research/senior-hunger-research/senior.

The United Methodist Church Discipleship Ministries. "The Dementia-Friendly Church." September 29, 2015. https://www.umcdiscipleship.org/resources/the-dementia-friendly-church.

The United Methodist Church Discipleship Ministries. "Equipping Leaders. Older Adults." https://www.umcdiscipleship.org/equipping-leaders/older-adults.

The United Methodist Church Discipleship Ministries. "Are Cafes the Leading Edge of Older-Adult Ministry?" August 28, 2015. https://www.umcdiscipleship.org/resources/are-cafes-the-leading-edge-of-older-adult-ministry.

The United Methodist Church Discipleship Ministries. "Equipping Leaders. Older Adults. 48 Older Adult Ministry Ideas." January 8, 2013. https://www.umcdiscipleship.org/resources/48-older-adult-ministry-ideas.

The United Methodist Church Discipleship Ministries. "Equipping Leaders. Older Adults. Elder Abuse: The Role of Church Leaders." September 10, 2010. https://www.umcdiscipleship.org/resources/elder-abuse-the-role-of-church-leaders.

U.S. Department of Justice. n.d. "Elder Abuse Statistics." https://www.justice.gov/file/970666/dl?inline=.

U.S. Department of Justice. 2019. "Red Flags of Elder Abuse." www.justice.gov, June 3, 2019. https://www.justice.gov/elderjustice/red-flags-elder-abuse.

U.S. Department of Justice Civil Rights Division. "ADA Standards for Accessible Design." ADA.gov. https://www.ada.gov/law-and-regs/design-standards/.

Bibliography

U.S. Department of Justice Civil Rights Division. "ADA Requirements: Effective Communication." February 28, 2020. https://www.ada.gov/resources/effective-communication/.

U.S. Department of Transportation. "Accessibility. ADA at DOT: Accessibility Initiatives." February 10, 2023. https://www.transportation.gov/accessibility.

USAgainstAlzheimers.org.

Weaver, Dr. Andrew J., and Dr. Harold G. Koenig. "Elder Abuse: A Faith-Based Response." *Ministry Magazine*, November 2003. https://www.ministrymagazine.org/archive/2003/11/elder-abuse-a-faith-based-response.html.

"WISQARS (Web-Based Injury Statistics Query and Reporting System)|Injury Center|CDC." 2020. www.cdc.gov, July 1, 2020. https://www.cdc.gov/injury/wisqars.

www.ingramcontent.com/pod-product-compliance
Lightning Source LLC
Chambersburg PA
CBHW071437150426
43191CB00008B/1159